*Edited by Pierre Joris
and Jerome Rothenberg*

André Breton: Selections. Edited and with an Introduction by Mark Polizzotti

María Sabina: Selections. Edited by Jerome Rothenberg. With Texts and Commentaries by Álvaro Estrada and Others

Paul Celan: Selections. Edited and with an Introduction by Pierre Joris

José Lezama Lima: Selections. Edited and with an Introduction by Ernesto Livon-Grosman

The publisher gratefully acknowledges the generous contribution to this book provided by the Literature in Translation Endowment Fund of the University of California Press Associates, which is supported by a major gift from Joan Palevsky.

PAUL CELAN: SELECTIONS

SELECTIONS

PAUL CELAN

EDITED AND WITH AN INTRODUCTION BY

PIERRE JORIS

UNIVERSITY OF CALIFORNIA PRESS

Berkeley Los Angeles London

University of California Press
Berkeley and Los Angeles, California

University of California Press, Ltd.
London, England

Acknowledgments of permissions begin on page 229.

Library of Congress Cataloging-in-Publication Data
Celan, Paul.
[Selections. English. 2005]
Paul Celan : selections / edited and with an introduction by Pierre Joris.
p.   cm. — (Poets for the millennium ; 3)
Includes bibliographical references.
ISBN 978-0-520-24168-8 (pbk. : alk.paper)
1. Celan, Paul — Translations into English.
2. Celan, Paul — Criticism and interpretation.
I. Joris, Pierre.   II. Title.   III. Series.
PT2605.E4A2   2005
831'.914 — dc22   2004000611

Manufactured in the United States of America
14   13   12   11   10   09   08
10   9   8   7   6   5   4   3

The paper used in this publication meets the minimum requirements of
ANSI/NISO Z39.48–1992 (R 1997) (*Permanence of Paper*).

CONTENTS

Introduction: "Polysemy without mask" 3

Key to Translators 37

POEMS

FROM Romanian Prose Poems (c. 1947)

As Partisan of Erotic Absolutism 41

FROM Mohn und Gedächtnis/Poppy and Memory (1952)

The Sand from the Urns 42

In Praise of Remoteness 43

Corona 44

Death Fugue 46

The Jars 48

Count the Almonds 49

FROM Von Schwelle zu Schwelle/From Threshold to Threshold (1955)

I Heard It Said 50

With a Variable Key 51

Shibboleth 52

Speak, You Too 54

The Vintagers 56

FROM Sprachgitter/Speech-Grille (1959)

Voices 58

Tenebrae 61

Speech-Grille 63

Matière de Bretagne 65

Stretto 67

FROM Die Niemandsrose/The Noonesrose (1963)

There Was Earth in Them 75

Zurich, Zum Storchen 76

Psalm 78

Tübingen, Jänner 79

Alchemical 81

Radix, Matrix 83

Blackearth 85

To One Who Stood at the Door 86

Mandorla 88

Siberian 89

The Syllable Pain 91

And with the Book from Tarussa 93

FROM Atemwende/Breathturn (1967)

You May 97

In the Rivers 97

To Stand 97

Threadsuns 98

Wordaccretion 98

Singable Remnant 99

No Sandart Anymore 100

Harbor 100

The Jugglerdrum 103

In Prague 103

Ashglory 104

The Written 105

Frihed 106

Solve 107

Coagula 108

Once 109

FROM Fadensonnen/Threadsuns (1968)

Frankfurt, September 110

Detour-/Maps 111

Spasms 112

Pau, Later 112

The Stallion 113

Lyon, Les Archers 114

The Industrious 115

When I Don't Know, Don't Know 116

You Were 117

Line the Wordcaves 117

Near, in the Aortic Arch 117

Imagine 118

FROM Lichtzwang/Lightduress (1970)

Soundscraps, Visionscraps 120

We Already Lay 120

Contact Mines 121

Cleared 121

Once 121

Two at Brancusi's 122

Todtnauberg 122

To a Brother in Asia 123

Oranienstrasse 1 124

Strew Ocher 124

Leap Centuries 125

Trek-Scow-Time 126

You Be Like You 127

FROM Schneepart/Snowpart (1971)

[CYCLE I]

Unwashed, Unpainted 128

You Lie 129

Lilac Air 130

Well-Graves 130

The Breached Year 131

Unreadability 131

Whorish Else 131

What Sews 132

I Hear the Axe Has Blossomed 133

With the Voice of the Fieldmouse 134

In Lizard 134

Snowpart 135

FROM Zeitgehöft/Timehalo (1976)

[CYCLE II: JERUSALEM POEMS]

Almonding You 136

It Stood 136

The Swelter 137

We Who Like the Seaoats Guard 137

A Ring, for Bowdrawing 138

The Radiance 138

Nitidous You 139

Come 140

A Bootfull of Brain 140

The Trumpet's Part 140

The Poles 141

The Kingsway 141

There Also 142

I Drink Wine 142

Something Shall Be 143

Nothingness 143

In the Bellshape 144

As I 144

Strangeness 144

Illuminated 145

PROSES

Conversation in the Mountains (1959) 149

The Meridian (1960) 154

DOCUMENTS

From the Correspondence

Letter #1: To Gisèle Celan-Lestrange (1952) 177

Letter #2: To Gisèle Celan-Lestrange (1952) 178

Letter #3: To Erich Einhorn (1962) 179

Letter #4: To Erich Einhorn (1962) 181

Letter #5: To René Char (unsent) (1962) 183

Letter #6: To Jean-Paul Sartre (unsent) (1962) 186

Letter #7: To Gisèle Celan-Lestrange (1965) 188

Letter #8: To Eric Celan (1968) 191

Letter #9: From Gisèle Celan-Lestrange to Paul (1969) 193

Letter #10: To Gisèle Celan-Lestrange (1970) 196

Das Stundenglas, tief *(facsimile)* 197

Über dich hinaus *(facsimile)* 198

Es wird etwas sein, später *(facsimile)* 199

ON PAUL CELAN

Paul Celan and Language

   Jacques Derrida 203

Encounters with Paul Celan

   E. M. Cioran 205

For Paul Celan

   Andrea Zanzotto 209

On Paul Celan in Neuchâtel

   Friedrich Dürrenmatt 215

The Memory of Words

   Edmond Jabès 217

Selected Bibliography 225

Acknowledgments of Permissions 229

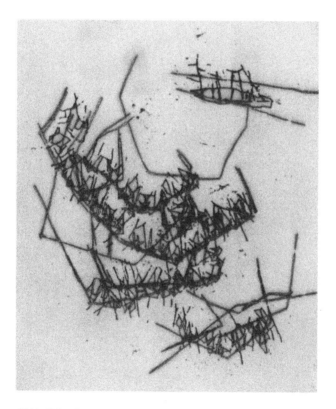

Gisèle Celan-Lestrange,
etching, *Je maintiendrai.*

"Polysemy without mask"

Thirty-four years after his death, Paul Celan's status as the greatest German-language poet of the second half of the twentieth century seems assured. His oeuvre — roughly 900 pages of poetry distributed over eleven volumes, 250 pages of prose, more than 1,000 pages of published correspondence, and nearly 700 pages of poetry translated from eight languages — has by now received massive critical attention, amounting to an astounding six thousand-plus entries, including reviews, essays, memoirs, and books in a dozen or more languages. And yet the work continues to be to a great extent terra incognita, a vast territory with uncertain, shifting borders, a map on which the unexplored sections by far outweigh the few areas that have been sketched in, reconnoitered.

Even of those textual areas crisscrossed repeatedly by various explorers, we have widely differing and often contradictory reports: it seems that every time a commentator ventures into an already mapped area, he or she returns with a new map charting different coordinates or a different topography for the same place. A Kafkaesque landscape and trek: the terrain the reader is confronted with appears simultaneously stony and amoebic, composed of multilayered strata continuously shifting in shape and consistency. It is so dense and multiple, in fact, that the various critical tunnels drilled into its layers never seem to cross or link up, constituting at best — that is, when the critic-explorer at least manages to get back home from the uncharted territories — a self-referential or self-interfering network of reticulated interconnections, often more relevant to the explorer's preoccupations than to the land under hand. It is an inexpugnable fortress, an unconquerable landscape, a "hyper-uranian" cosmos.

Why do such geostrategic, quasi-military images and metaphors so readily come to mind when one gropes toward a comprehension and description of Celan and his oeuvre? No doubt the poems themselves, their vocabulary, their syntactical gnarledness, their textual strategies, tactical evasiveness, and philological ruses, propose and even demand such a reading. But the life itself seems to fit such a description: mapped out spatially, it describes an encirclement of Germany, originating in Czernowitz and moving through Bucharest and Vienna to Paris, from where Celan undertakes a number of quick, short raids across the borders into that country. Two of the people he considered his real friends and associates were in fact strategically situated on "meridians" he himself could not inhabit and which helped him to encircle Germany: Osip Mandelstam (the "brother," on whom more later) in Russia and Nelly Sachs (the "sister" poet) in Sweden. I use the military metaphor advisedly, for there seems to me to run through Celan's life if not a desire for assault on Germany and revenge for the death of his parents (or rather of his mother) then at least a constant, unrelenting feeling of being under attack and needing to counter this attack.

The Celanian dynamic is, however, not simple-minded or one-directional: it involves a complex double movement — to use the terms of Empedocles — of *philotes* (love) for his mother('s tongue) and *neikos* (strife) against her murderers who are the originators and carriers of that same tongue. He is caught in this love/strife dynamic, the common baseline or ground of which (as *Grund,* ground, but also and simultaneously as *Abgrund,* abyss) is the German language, irrevocably binding together both the murdered and the murderer, a dynamic that structures all of Celan's thinking and writing.

But the critics' problems are specific to their undertaking (i.e., their need to prove that the methodologies they are invested in are the right ones and will result in the "true" interpretation of the poem) and should not discourage the reader. It is important to state at the outset that if Celan's poems are often difficult (and get more opaque in the late work) they are not incomprehensible. Celan himself, when asked about the difficulties of the poems, insisted that they were in no way hermetic and that all one had to do was to read them again and again. At the same time he claimed a necessary opacity for poetry today, first because the poem is "dunkel" (dark, obscure) because of its thingness, its phenomenality. In a note toward his essay "The Meridian" he writes: "Regarding the darkness of the poem today, imagination and experience, experience and imagination let me think of a darkness of the poem *qua* poem, of a constitutive, even congenital darkness. In other words: the poem is born dark; the result of a radical individuation, it is born as a piece of language, as far as language manages to be world, is loaded with world."[1]

And this world-making, this making of a new world through and in poetry, is what I want to insist on, lest the above description of Celan's relation to Germany would tend to elide the desire for "making it new" and limit Celan's work to a revenge play. It is just that for Celan, as survivor, the poetry that will be — that has to be — written after Auschwitz has to always remain conscious of — *eingedenk* — the

---

1. Paul Celan, *Der Meridian, Endfassung, Vorstufen, Materialien,* edited by Bernhard Böschenstein and Heino Schmull, Tübinger Ausgabe (Frankfurt am Main: Suhrkamp Verlag, 1999), 84.

horror of the Shoah. If the past is the abyss and simultaneously the ground on which the work rests, the stance it will take is, however, resolutely forward looking and hopeful (except perhaps in some of the bitter late poems written under the psychic pressure of mental illness). It will certainly not deny the possibility of a new world, of a new and more human age. In early 1946 the American poet Charles Olson suggested in his poem "La Préface" that one world age had come to an end, an age, or *yuga*, that stretched from the prehistoric caves (among the major discoveries in relation to art of the twentieth century) to the concentration camps: "Buchenwald   new Altamira cave/With a nail they drew the object of the hunt." By implication, Olson was simultaneously making the claim for a new age, to begin after Buchenwald. "We are born" he writes, "not of the buried but of these unburied dead" — an eerie echo of Celan's "Death Fugue" in which the "we" of the survivors "scoop[s] out a grave in the sky where it's roomy to lie." All poetry, after that date, will have to be, at some level, a poetry of witnessing. But it cannot stop there if it wants to be of essential use, as both Olson and Celan insist; it cannot simply bear witness to the past but must at the same time be resolutely turned to the future: it has to be open, it has to be imaginatively engaged in the construction of a new world, it has to look forward, to be visionary. It is that forward looking, that vertical stance that I also hear in Celan's question about bearing witness for the witness. Celan's work is that of both a witness and a visionary.[2]

2. This combination — witness and visionary — is not as rare as it would seem in our times. Ammiel Alcalay, for example, speaks in the same terms of the Moroccan poet Abdellatif Laâbi in his foreword to Laâbi's volume of selected poems, *The World's Embrace* (San Francisco: City Lights, 2003).

A word more needs to be said about the mode of Celan's witnessing, as it differs markedly from that of other Holocaust writers, and that difference itself is what makes possible the visionary stance I am so insistent about. Despite the presence throughout the work (or better maybe, below the work) of the events of the Nazi years, especially the murder of his mother, there is a strong refusal in Celan to let his writing become simply a repository for a narrative of the Shoah, in profound contrast to most Holocaust writers, a major part of whose endeavor has been to dwell again and again on the past in order to chronicle with as much accuracy as they could muster the events of their lives during those fateful years (Elie Wiesel and Primo Levi come to mind but also poets like Abba Kovener or Abraham Sutzkever). Not only did Celan not write such an autobiographical prosopopoeia, but, according to all accounts, he refused steadfastly to speak in public or in private about the events of his life connected with the Shoah. Symptomatic for this reticence is the following biographical comment from 1949: "With the exception of a one-year stay in France, I, for all practical purposes, never left my native city prior to 1941. I don't need to relate what the life of a Jew was like during the war years." This decision not to relate, not to dwell on those years — no matter how much they shaped his early life, no matter the shadow they threw on the rest of his life — informed the stance of his writing for the next quarter century. One way to see this is to examine his rewriting of "Death Fugue" in the poem "Stretto," which I do later in this introduction. But let me now turn to a closer look at Paul Celan's life, before addressing some of the issues his poetry raises.

Celan was born Paul Antschel in Czernowitz, capital of the Bukovina, in 1920. He was raised in a Jewish family which insisted that young Paul receive the best secular education, with his mother inculcating her love of the German language and culture, and also that he remain firm in his Jewish roots: both his parents came from solid orthodox and, on one side, Hasidic backgrounds. His father had strong Zionist convictions, and his mother, notwithstanding her great admiration for classical German culture, kept the Jewish tradition alive in the household on a daily basis: it was a kosher household in which the Sabbath candles were conscientiously lit every week. In this, the Antschels were not very different from most of the more than fifty thousand Jews of Czernowitz during the tail end of those "golden years" for Bukovina Jewry — years that started under the benign though calculating Austrian-Hungarian regime with the "emancipation" of the Jews in 1867 and began to decline after the fall of the Hapsburg monarchy in 1918 and the incorporation of the Bukovina into Romania, the government of which immediately began to try to "romanize" the province, though with relatively little success. Czernowitz retained its "pulsing Jewish life which resisted all anti-Semitic attempts to undermine it" until 1940.[3]

In November 1938 Celan traveled by train from Czernowitz to Paris via Berlin, where he arrived at a fateful moment — the morning after Kristallnacht — later remembered in a poem set by its title in Paris ("La Contrescarpe") but alluding to the stopover in Berlin:

Via Krakow
you came, at the Anhalter
railway station
a smoke flowed towards your glance,
it already belonged to tomorrow.

3. Much of the information for this section is indebted to Israel Chalfen's *Paul Celan: A Biography of His Youth* (New York: Persea Books, 1991) and to Wolfgang Emmerich's *Paul Celan* (Reinbek by Hamburg: Rowohlt, 1999).

In summer 1939 Celan returned to Czernowitz after his first year as a medical student at the University of Tours. The Hitler-Stalin Pact in August of that year put Romania on a war footing, and any return to studies in France became impossible. In spring 1940 the Soviet Union addressed an ultimatum to the Romanian government, demanding the immediate handing over of Bessarabia and North Bukovina. Romania, powerless and unable to expect any support from its theoretical allies, France and England, who were themselves now under attack from Hitler, handed over both provinces. On June 28 Soviet troops entered Czernowitz. The first year of occupation by foreign troops was relatively peaceful, but on June 13, 1941, the citizens of Czernowitz got a first inkling of the horrors to come. In a single night the NKVD arrested four thousand men, women, and children and deported them to Siberia. Then, on June 22, Hitler attacked the Soviet Union. On the southern front German troops reinforced by Romanian units pushed the Soviets back and occupied the Bukovina and Czernowitz (Antonescu, the Romanian dictator, had enthusiastically joined the German-Italian-Japanese axis in November 1940).

The retreating Soviet troops helped their own civilians — bureaucrats and party officials who had joined the occupation troops — to evacuate the Bukovina, but only just before the last train was ready to leave, reports Israel Chalfen, did they make the rather lukewarm suggestion that the general population of Czernowitz should flee to Russia. Only a few committed Communists followed suit, among them Paul Celan's close friend Erich Einhorn. On July 5, 1941, the Romanian troops occupied Czernowitz, and the German Einsatz–Truppe D, led by SS-Brigadeführer Ohlendorf, reached the city the very next day. The SS had one essential job to fulfill — "Energisch durchgreifen, die Juden liquidieren," to energetically liquidate the Jews — as they did not trust the Romanians to do it thoroughly enough. On July 7 the Great Temple went up in flames, and for the next three days the hunt was open: 682 Jews were murdered. By late August Ohlendorf triumphantly reported to Berlin that more than 3,000 had been killed. On October 11 the ghetto was created — the first one in the history of the Bukovina and of Czernowitz. Then began the "Umsiedlung" (relocation) of most Jews to Transnistria. The Romanians managed to argue with the Germans and to retain 15,000 Jews in Czernowitz to keep the city functioning. The Antschel family were among those who, at least for the time being, remained in the ghetto. Paul was ordered to forced labor on construction sites. Then, in June 1942, a new wave of arrests and deportations began, taking place primarily on Saturday nights. With the help of his friend Ruth Lackner, Paul had found a large and comfortable hideout, but his parents refused adamantly to take refuge there, preferring to remain in their own house — where Celan's mother prepared rucksacks in case they should be deported. On one of those Saturday nights, disobeying his parents' orders, Paul left the house and spent the night in the hideout. When he returned the next morning he found his home sealed off: his parents had been deported.

Celan continued to work in forced labor camps, hauling stones and debris from the Prut River for the reconstruction of a bridge. In late fall 1942 a letter (probably from his mother) brought the news that his father, physically broken by the slave labor he was subjected to, had died — either shot by the SS or succumbing to typhus; the exact cause of death was never established. Later that winter the news that his mother too had been killed by the Nazis reached him via an escaped family member. Paul himself was now sent to a forced labor camp some four hundred miles south of Czernowitz, where he remained throughout the next year until the labor camps were closed in February 1944. In April Soviet troops occupied Czernowitz without a fight. Celan was put to work as a medical auxiliary in a psychiatric clinic and made one trip as an ambulance assistant to Kiev. Another year was spent at the university in Czernowitz, now studying English literature (he had already started translating poems by Shakespeare during the years in the forced labor camps). While making a living translating newspaper articles from Romanian for a Ukrainian newspaper, he put together two manuscripts of his poems, an act that clearly affirmed his decision to become (or remain) a German-language poet.

Celan left his hometown for good in April 1945 to move to Bucharest, the capital of Romania, where he found work as a translator of Russian literature into Romanian. He also translated a number of short stories by Franz Kafka, an author who was to remain of central importance to him for the rest of his life. He started to engage in a life devoted to writing, gathering and reworking the early Bukovinan poems, writing new ones and beginning to publish. It is also at this time that he changed his name from Antschel to Celan. He sought out the most influential Bukovinan poet of the time, Alfred Margul-Sperber, who welcomed him warmly, and met Petre Solomon, who was to remain a lifelong friend. A relatively happy time, then, but one always framed by the dark past and an uncertain present and future. The work of those years is tinged with investigations of surrealism, as is most obvious in the prose poems in Romanian (the only time he used a language other than German) he wrote during that period, one of which opens the poetry section of this book.

Then, in December 1947, he clandestinely crossed over to Vienna — from the little we know, a harrowing journey on foot from Romania through Hungary to Austria. The only German-speaking place the poet was ever to live in, the Vienna of those years[4] — Orson Wells's *The Third Man* comes close to what it must have felt like to Celan — was relatively hospitable to the young poet, though the minimal and superficial denazification program it had submitted itself to must have left the survivor uneasy, to say the least. Through an introduction from Margul-Sperber he met Otto Basil, editor of the avant-garde literary magazine *Der Plan,* in which he would publish a number of poems, and at some point he went to meet Ludwig von Ficker, who had been a close friend of Georg Trakl's and who celebrated the young Bukovinan poet as "heir to Else Lasker-Schüler." The meeting with the surrealist painter Edgar Jené led to the writing of the first essay by Celan we have, "Edgar Jené and the Dream of the Dream," composed as a foreword to a Jené exhibition catalog. He also met people who were to remain lifelong friends, such as Nani and Klaus Demus, and maybe most important, the young poet Ingeborg Bachman, who — even after their early love affair faded — remained a close friend and staunch defender in the later, darker days of the Goll affair. He readied his first book, *The Sand from the Urns,* for publication — though he would recall the book and have it destroyed, judging that the many typos and mistakes lethally disfigured his work. But Celan clearly did not find what he was looking for, and even before his first book came out he left Vienna for Paris, where he arrived in July 1948 and where he would remain until his death in late April 1970.

From Hölderlin's hallucinatory walk to the Bordelais and back, to von Horvath's strange death (a branch severed by lightning killed

---

4. For a detailed account of those years, see *Displaced: Paul Celan in Wien, 1947–1949,* edited by Peter Gossen and Marcus G. Patka (Frankfurt am Main: Suhrkamp Verlag, 2001).

him on the Champs Elysées), France has always proved a point of focal, not to say fatal, attraction — and certainly often enough, a point of rupture — for poets and writers of the German language: suffice it to mention in this context the names of Heinrich Heine, Rainer Maria Rilke, and Walter Benjamin. For most of these, the stay in France was limited and freely chosen. But often also their residence was a matter of political or intellectual exile. Few of them, however, had as symbiotic and long-term a relationship with France as Paul Celan.

Once settled in Paris, and despite the rather normal early difficulties, Celan began to make contact with the literary scene and soon met a good number of writers who were to stay important for him. Among them was the poet Yves Bonnefoy, who recalls Celan in those days:

> His gestures, above all in the first years after Vienna — at the time of the room in *rue des Ecoles,* of the cheap university restaurants, of the archaic typewriter with a Greek-temple peristyle, of destitution — had nonchalance, and his head had a graceful movement towards the shoulder: as if to accompany, for a stretch, along the summer streets after a lively night's conversation, the friend being left for a whole day.[5]

It was Bonnefoy who introduced Celan, on the latter's insistence, to Yvan Goll in November 1949. This encounter would much later produce terrible results: festering throughout the fifties, the "Goll affair" — Claire Goll, the poet's widow, falsely accused Celan of plagiarism, and, shockingly, a range of German newspapers and reviews

5. Yves Bonnefoy, "Paul Celan," in *Translating Tradition: Paul Celan in France,* ed. Benjamin Hollander (San Francisco: *ACTS* 8/9, 1988): 12.

uncritically accepted and spread those false accusations—broke in 1960 and does indeed mark a traumatic turning point.[6]

Celan does not seem ever to have seriously thought about moving elsewhere and certainly not after meeting the French graphic artist Gisèle Lestrange in fall 1951 and marrying her in late 1952.[7] Celan became a naturalized French citizen in 1955, and it was as a French citizen and a Parisian literary personality that he spent the rest of his life, employed as a teacher of German language and literature at the Ecole Normale Supérieure on the rue d'Ulm, summering from 1962 on in the little farmhouse the Celans bought in Normandy. His first child, François, died shortly after birth in 1953, but 1955 saw the birth of his son, Eric, with whom Celan would be very close. The last years saw a separation from his wife and son, and from 1967 to 1970 Celan lived alone in Paris. His 1969 trip to Israel clearly was not an attempt to leave France behind: he broke that trip off after two weeks to return precipitately to Paris.

And yet to this day and despite the massiveness of the *Sekundärliteratur* around Celan, relatively little has been written about this relationship with his adopted country.[8] German scholars tend to analyze Celan's work in the context of what one could describe as a

6. For a full treatment of this affair, see Barbara Wiedemann, ed., *Paul Celan—Die Goll-Affäre* (Frankfurt am Main: Suhrkamp Verlag, 2000).

7. For the relationship between Paul Celan and Gisèle Celan-Lestrange, see the recently published correspondence in two volumes: Paul Celan, Gisèle Celan-Lestrange, *Correspondance,* edited and with commentary by Bertrand Badiou, with assistance from Eric Celan (Paris: Editions du Seuil, 2001).

8. The only serious attempt to date to assess the relation of Celan with France is issue 8/9 of *ACTS* (1988), edited by Benjamin Hollander and titled *Translating Tradition: Paul Celan in France.* See also my essay "Celan and France" (on which I draw for the following pages), in *Contretemps* 2, May 2001. http://www.usyd.edu .au/contretemps/dir/contents.html.

nearly nationalistic "Germanistik" tradition, at best footnoting his relationship to France as a contingent aspect of his life and work. Two of the best-known and standard texts on German poetry after 1945 will serve as examples: while an essay by Klaus Weissenberger at least mentions that Celan lived in France most of his life, Otto Knörrich's otherwise fine essay does not give the slightest indication of the biogeographic complexity of Celan's life. Weissenberger's compilation has introductory chapters organized according to geographic principles (BRD, DDR, Austria, Switzerland). Joseph Strelka, who wrote the chapter on Austrian poetry, seems to include Celan implicitly but, again, essentially as an influence on Austrian poetry and without other biogeographic references, except for the mention of Celan's birthplace. Just as limiting, or error inducing, can be the often used categorial description of Celan as "Exil-Dichter": in exile indeed, but from where?

The figure that emerges is baffling: Celan is loudly proclaimed as one of the greatest if not the greatest "German poet" of the century (since Rilke, or Trakl, or George, depending on the given author's preferences), when in fact he was a naturalized French citizen of Jewish-Bukovinan descent who never lived on German soil, though he wrote (nearly) all his life in his mother's language, German. The correspondence with his wife shows that Celan was a superb writer in French, and had he decided to write at least some of his work in that language (or even translate his own work into French), no doubt the French could and most likely would have claimed him as one of their own — as they did, for example, with Samuel Beckett, Tristan Tzara, Eugene Ionesco, and, more to the point, E. M. Cioran and Gherasim Luca. That he did not do this is of course essential but needs to be analyzed and contextualized within the complex relationships he entertained with his mother's tongue and his harsh, nearly hysterical strictures against poets attempting to write in a language other than the mother tongue. Celan, this most proficient multilingual poet, returned to this theme several times, the strongest formulation being reported by Ruth Lackner, to whom he said: "Only in the mother tongue can one speak one's own truth, in a foreign language the poet lies."[9] Later, in 1961, he formulated the quandary again, as an answer to a questionnaire, "The Problem of the Bilingual," from the Flinker Bookshop in Paris:

> I do not believe there is such a thing as bilingual poetry. Double-talk, yes, this you may find among our various contemporary arts and acrobatics of the word, especially those who manage to establish themselves in blissful harmony with each fashion of consumer culture, being as polyglot as they are polychrome. Poetry is by necessity a unique instance of language. Hence never — forgive the truism, but poetry, like truth, goes all too often to the dogs — hence never what is double.[10]

A word needs to be said here about Celan as translator, the activity he was perhaps most involved in besides his own writing, and one that should not be seen as secondary because it is an integral part of his poetics and of his oeuvre (if one subtracts a number of translations, mainly of novels, done for purely financial reasons). The complete edition of Celan's poetry translations takes up two volumes of the *Collected Works* (indicating that Celan translated the work of forty-three poets over the years); the first one of these consists of some four hundred pages of translations from the French. Looking at this work chronologically, it is clear that the young Celan was still very much under the sway of surrealism. The first poets he translated, probably

9. Chalfen, *Paul Celan,* 148.

10. Paul Celan, *Collected Prose,* translated by Rosmarie Waldrop (Manchester: Carcanet Press 1986), 23.

still in the late forties, were André Breton, Aimé Césaire, Henri Pastoureau, and Benjamin Péret. (Eluard and Desnos would be added to this list in the late fifties.) Throughout the fifties, Celan's translations show a serious, not to say systematic, investigation of French poetry, reaching back to the fathers of modernism, Baudelaire, Nerval, Mallarmé, Apollinaire, Valéry (whose "Young Fate" — a poem Rilke thought untranslatable — he translated, he told a friend, so as to gain the right to be critical of that kind of art), and especially Rimbaud, whose *Bateau Ivre* Celan rendered magisterially into German. How the work of translation is at the same time an important "exercise" — and indeed more than an exercise — for honing his own poetics is made clear in Bernard Böschenstein's commentary on the Rimbaud translation:

> Rimbaud's poem offered him a chance to creatively follow his inclination toward a strange and specialized vocabulary. He took note, with satisfaction, of finds such as *Derweil die Tide tobte* (meanwhile the tide raged) or *sie fahren nicht, die Klipper, die Koggen, die mich suchten* (they don't set sail, the clippers, the cogs that sought me) for *les moniteurs et les voiliers des Hanses* (the monitors and sailboats of the Hanses).[11]

Besides work by René Char and Henri Michaux, personal connections and his involvement with the magazine *L'Ephémère* led him to translate younger French poets such as André du Bouchet and Jean Daive during the sixties.

If he also translated a range of poets from English (twenty-one Shakespearean sonnets and ten poems by Emily Dickinson representing the bulk of that work), Italian (a dozen poems by Guiseppe

---

11. Bernard Böschenstein, "Paul Celan and French Poetry" (translated from the German by Joel Golb), in *Translating Tradition*, 182.

Ungaretti), Portuguese (Fernando Pessoa, with the help of Edouard Roditi), Romanian (Gellu Naum and Tudoor Argezi, most notably) and Hebrew (David Rokeah), it is Celan's work from Russian that is most important. He had learned Russian as a student in Czernowitz and always felt strong affinities with that language. In 1957 he turned again toward Russian and started gathering a good library of modern Russian literature, especially poetry. He translated Alexander Blok's masterpiece, "The Twelve," a volume of poems by Sergey Yesenin, and work by Velimir Khlebnikov and Yevgeni Yevtushenko. But the poet he certainly felt closest to in terms of his own poetics was Osip Mandelstam, in whom he saw a double of himself — a persecuted Jewish poet with socialist leanings, sent into exile, who died in the gulag near Vladivostok in 1938. A poet of whom one could say — as of Celan too — that, in Antonin Artaud's words for van Gogh, he was "suicided by society." Celan dedicated his 1963 volume, *Die Niemandsrose,* to Mandelstam. His identification with the Russian poet was such that in several letters to friends he described himself as "Pawel Lwowitsch Tselan/Russkij poët in partibus nemetskich infidelium/s'ist nur ein Jud" — Paul Celan/Russian poet in the lands of German infidels/'tis only a Jew.

And yet despite the evident multiculturalism and multilingualism, throughout his life Celan saw himself as part of "German" literature, wanted his *work* to be a visible presence in that country, wanted it to have an impact on German letters. But this desire is more ambiguous than has been suggested so far, and may be closer to the love/strife dynamic I described earlier. The pathos, mentioned by people close to him in France, of Celan, day after day, on a bench in Paris going through the German papers to find out if there was mention of him but also afraid that this mention might be negative, worried that someone somewhere was preparing an attack on him, is not the nostalgic pathos of the expatriate, happy for any scrap of news in the old language from the old country, but that of a deeply wounded man, hoping that the strategies of his solitary struggle are paying off. The same worries and fear were even more apparent on those occasions when Celan would leave Paris to travel to Germany for readings, as he did on many occasions from 1952 on. The fear of and profound mistrust in Germany, even after the defeat of the Third Reich, has often been read (and all too easily dismissed) as misplaced and ungrounded, and thus as nothing more than paranoia and a symptom of the incipient psychic disorder that was to darken his later years. That Celan was extremely sensitive to even the slightest whiff of anti-Semitism is indeed true — and should be seen as a positive attribute rather than dismissed as paranoia, that is, delusion. In his case, I would submit, William Burroughs's dictum that "a paranoid is a man who knows the facts" holds true. Celan knew whereof he was speaking when he called the new Germany an "Angstlandschaft," a landscape of fear.[12] Here is how Wolfgang Emmerich describes the situation in Germany during those years, a description that leaves no doubt that Celan's perceptions were not unfounded:

> Right after the foundation [of the new German state] in 1949 a law exempting Nazi criminals from punishment was enacted, and in 1950 the denazification program set up by the Allied forces was terminated. In 1951 thousands of "state workers" — judges, public prosecutors, policemen, army officers, teachers, professors — were allowed by

---

12. See Theo Buck, *Muttersprache, Mördersprache,* Celan-Studien I (Aachen: Rimbaud, 1993), 159. (Cited by Wolfgang Emmerich.)

law to reintegrate public service. Consequently the legal system, the administration and education were tilted for another two decades towards assuaging and repressing the Nazi past. . . . Worse happened: the reemergence and rise of the NS elites who had taken part in the preparation of mass crimes[,] . . . hundreds of men who had for example been Gestapo heads and commando leaders. To begin with they joined together socially, in the main undisturbed by the justice system, as "circles," "regulars" or "clubs," until many of them managed to regain posts of responsibility in the economy and the legal system. Besides this opportunism, there came provocation: In 1960 already the police recorded over 600 cases of swastika and slogan graffiti, mainly on synagogues.[13]

Celan had indeed actual, factual reason to be worried. That the new Germany had not shed some of the old blindness he also knew from personal experience. His first reading trip to Germany in 1952 had been under the aegis of Gruppe 47, an association of young German writers, which had invited him on the recommendation of his friends Milo Dor and Ingeborg Bachman to their reunion in Niendorf. Although none of the group were old Nazis, most of them had spent some years of their youth as German soldiers, and their easygoing fraternity-like camaraderie, based on shared wartime memories and experiences, must have felt very alien to the young Jew from the Bukovina. Celan, in the quiet and meditative manner that would be the hallmark of all his readings, read "Death Fugue" — to very mixed reactions. He later described the event to his friend Hermann Lenz in the following words: "Oh well, those soccer players. . . . So then someone said to me: The poems you read struck me as quite unpleasant. On top of it, you read them with the voice of

13. Emmerich, *Paul Celan*, 106.

Goebbels."[14] Celan felt just as put out by the positive critical reception of the early work, especially that of "Death Fugue"; thus, for example, did the poet and critic Hans Egon Holthusen — who had been an enthusiastic member of the SS before the fall of the Reich — claim in his essay "Five Young German Poets" (published in the very highly regarded and influential magazine *Der Merkur*) that Celan's poem "escapes the bloody horror chamber of history" to "rise to the ethereal domain of pure poetry," via a "dreamy," "surreal" and "transcendent" language. This negation of the content of the poem was not a singular aberrance but happened with regularity throughout the fifties and sixties. When the by now world-famous poem was printed in German school anthologies, the accompanying suggestions for class discussion exclusively queried the poem's formal aspects — avoiding any discussion of its explicit content. And yet Celan would return again and again to read his work in Germany in those quick forays I spoke of above. In 1967, for example, he read in Freiburg im Brisgau and then went to visit the philosopher Martin Heidegger (who admired Celan's work and had been at the reading) to ask him, as the poem written on that occasion has it, " for a hope, today,/for a thinker's/word/to come,/ in the heart," that is, for some explanation or apology for the philosopher's involvement with the Nazi regime, or for his total and deafening silence concerning the Shoah in the years after the war. On that occasion too, no explanation, no apology was forthcoming — only an inability on the philosopher's part to understand the sharply critical poem Celan wrote about the aborted meeting and sent him a few months later (see p. 122).

14. Hermann Lenz, "Erinnerungen an Paul Celan," in *Paul Celan,* edited by Werner Hamacher and Winfried Menninghaus (Frankfurt am Main: Suhrkamp Verlag, 1988), 316.

A wounded and psychically exhausted Celan would return to Paris from these various expeditions into Germany. There is little doubt that life in the French capital was far more livable, though not exactly easy either for Celan, whose cultural background, that specific mixture of *Mitteleuropa* and *Ostjudentum*, did not fit perfectly with Gallic modes of being. In a letter to Edith Silberman he described Paris as "leider, ein sehr, sehr hartes Pflaster" (unhappily a very, very hard place).[15] The poet Yves Bonnefoy, in the memoir of Celan, relates the following incident:

> I can still hear Paul Celan saying to me one afternoon, when we got together to talk about Romanesque architecture and painting, *you* (meaning French or Western poets) *are at home inside your reference points and language. But I'm outside.*[16]

Bonnefoy sees this statement as expressing Celan's condition as a *"Jew with an unpronounceable name* in wartime Europe (and after), a Germanophone in Paris," believing that "doubtlessly the most harshly felt form of his exile was that as a Jew, i.e., inhabited by a founding word from the *other,* moving outward from I to thou, he had to live in the essential impersonality of the Western languages, which only conceive incarnation in terms of paradox and on the basis of a borrowed book."[17] Celan's exile is absolute: he is, to use a French phrase, "un mort en sursis." To blame his chosen place of residence for this fact will not do. To consider France as the least painful place for this man to "live out" the undue supplement that he considered his own life after the Holocaust

15. Edith Silberman, "Erinnerungen an Paul Celan," in *Argumentum e Silentio: International Paul Celan Symposium 1984* (Berlin: W. de Gruyter, 1987), 441.

16. Bonnefoy, "Paul Celan," 12.

17. Ibid.; original emphasis.

and his mother's death seems closer to the truth. Paris, then, for Celan, was a place to be used as an outpost from which to keep one watchful eye (a northeasterly meridian) on Germany and one mourning eye (a southeasterly meridian) on the deathscape of his homeland.

The last decade of Celan's life was overshadowed by repeated bouts of mental illness, a result no doubt of the traumas experienced during the Nazi years but triggered and sharpened by the Goll affair. His illness demanded a number of voluntary stays in psychiatric clinics, during which he was subjected to intense medication and on several occasions to drug and shock therapy. I have spoken in more detail of those stays and their relation to the poetry written during that time in the introduction to my translation of *Threadsuns* and refer the reader to that volume[18] and, more important, to the Celan–Celan-Lestrange correspondence, which is the best, albeit still incomplete, record we have to date concerning the events of those years.[19]

As a survivor of that deathscape the French call the "univers concentrationaire," Celan cannot but bear witness, though the mode of this witnessing differs vastly from that of most survivors while simultaneously radically differing in relation to itself over time. Let us now investigate this difference in Celan's poetics from his early poetry to his later, mature poetics by looking more closely at "Death Fugue" —

18. Paul Celan, *Threadsuns* (Los Angeles: Sun & Moon Press, 2000; Copenhagen: Green Integer, 2004).

19. After I wrote this introduction, and thus too late to take it into account, Mme Viviane Jabès Crasson sent me an essay by Steven Jaron that is one of the only serious attempts to deal with Celan's psychic condition that I know of: "Morceaux de sommeil, coins: Une réflexion autour de Paul Celan et Gisèle Celan-Lestrange," in *L'ombre de l'image de la falsification à l'infigurable,* edited by Murielle Gagnebin (Seyssel: Editions Champ Vallon, 2003), 262–81.

written at the latest in early 1945 but in all probability already completed in late 1944. This positions it as one of the early "mature" poems of the young Celan, preceded only by the youthful poems — mainly love lyrics, though they already contain the darkness and preoccupation with death that became the hallmark of the later Celan — gathered by Ruth Kraft as *Gedichte 1938–1944*, published in 1985. When he published it for the first time, in a Romanian magazine and in Romanian translation, the poem was still called "Todestango." When he included it in *The Sand from the Urns*, it appeared as the closing poem — clearly to mark its special place, though not its chronological situation. In his first real book, *Poppy and Memory*, published in 1952, "Death Fugue" is located at the very center, surrounded by poems that in the main postdate it.

I have already discussed Celan's later uneasy relationship to this poem and his decision not to allow it to be anthologized any further or to be read at public readings. But there is also, I believe, a decision not to let himself be identified with that single, early work — this on at least two levels. First, Celan was loath to be made a mouthpiece for what came to be called Holocaust poetry and refused to narrativize his experiences from that period — though what has been called the "ontological shame" of the survivor must also have an important role to play in this context. Second, as a poet, Celan did not want "Death Fugue" to overshadow the rest of his work, especially as this early poem can be read as an exception in his work and not as paradigmatic for his mature poetics. At the same time, his refusal to allow the poem to be published in later anthologies coincides more or less with a second critical turn away from or even against his work (after the early dismissal by misreading at the hands Hans Egon Holthusen and others) in Germany where, from the volume *Speech-Grille* onward, complaints about the growing obscurity and hermeticism of the work are coincident with and amplified by the rise of a new generation of German poets, such as Jürgen Theobaldy or Rolf Dieter Brinkmann, who tried to define their own poetics in opposition to both the "hermetic" poetry and the "Naturlyrik" of the first postwar generation (Günter Eich and Karl Krolow, among others) and who, influenced by U.S. poetry and events such as the Vietnam War and the growing student movement, see themselves as concerned with a different set of values and problems.

The tension surrounding his relationship with "Death Fugue" can be seen as emblematic of the tension in Celan with regard to two essential poles: on the one hand, the need to witness, and, on the other, the desire I earlier spoke of as "visionary," to create in and through the poems a new, viable world that would overcome the past — without abolishing or dismissing it. This tension could be traced schematically in Celan's oeuvre if one were to look at the first part of it as an attempt to witness and to look at the late work, starting with *Breathturn* if not already with *Die Niemandsrose,* as essentially concerned with the very possibility of creating such a new world — at least in and through poetry.

The reason why "Death Fugue," as against the late poetry, exercises such a fascination and is so "readable" is essentially that its poetics are still rather traditional: the relationship between word and world, between signifier and signified, is not put into question. It is a poem that still, somehow, maybe desperately, believes, or wants to believe, or acts as if it did believe, in the fullness of utterance, in the possibility of representation. This fullness of language presupposes a fullness of being, a being who speaks and in whom both language and what language talks about are grounded. As against nearly all of Celan's subsequent poetry, the one thing not questioned in "Death Fugue" is the one who speaks and the place from which that one speaks. The poem is written (or spoken) by a "survivor" who adopts the persona of a "wir," who speaks in the name of a "wir," the "we," of the murdered Jews: "Black milk ... *we* drink you at dusktime/*we* drink you at noontime and dawntime we drink you at night/*we* drink and drink/*we* scoop out a grave in the sky."

That the dead can speak, or that a "survivor" can speak for them, that there can be a witnessing to their death, this is what Celan is going to radically put into question. The poem "Stretto" (p. 67), written in 1958, is in many ways a rewriting of "Death Fugue" — down to the musical theme, as the word *stretto* (*Engführung* in German) means literally a narrowing and comes from the technical vocabulary of fugal composition. The poem expands its landscape of disaster to include Hiroshima, but there is no more direct reference to the Shoah, no more "Meister from Germany," for example. The poem starts: "Verbracht ins/Gelände/mit der untrüglichen Spur: // Gras auseinandergeschrieben. Die Steine, weiss" (Brought into/the terrain/with the unmistakable spoor: // grass written asunder. The stones, white). We no longer know who speaks, who is being addressed; the landscape can be, and is, simultaneously an inner and an outer landscape. On one level we can read these opening lines as indicating the situation of the reader coming to this difficult poem; on another level it is the "inner landscape" of the poet's mind/psyche; and on a third level it is also and simultaneously the landscape of his parents' death, the "Gelände," the terrain into which they were "verbracht" (the prefix *ver-* here brings the word into resonance with *Verbrechen*, meaning "crime"; an English construction that could carry some of that charge would be, instead of the verb *to bring*, the verb *to place* with the negatively loaded prefix *dis-*, thus "displaced into"). The same can be said for the opening verses of the next stanza: "The place where they lay, it has/a name — it has/no name. They did not lie there."

The problematics of the poem include, in an unstated way, the mass annihilation of human beings from Auschwitz to Hiroshima but in combination with another problematics, that of speaking, of saying itself, and, by extension, that of the possibility of the poem itself. The fourth stanza, for example, plays on *Wort* (word), which is the most often repeated and questioned ("heraufbeschwört," to use a Celanian term) word in the Celan opus, and, contrapuntally, the words *ashes* and *night*. Where the poet-narrator-reader of the "Todesfuge" had his mouth full of words, in the "Engführung" what is most fully present is absence. We are, cosmically speaking, in a vast empty space traversed by "Partikelngestöber" — particle flurries, reminiscent of Celan's later coinage "Metapherngestöber," metaphor flurries.

The only place or object the poet finds to address his speaking to is the stone: "there was time, to try it with the stone — it remained hospitable, it didn't interrupt" (lit. it didn't "ins Wort fallen," "fall into, upon the word"). The stone that is addressed reappears in another seminal poem, "Radix, Matrix," from the volume *Die Niemandsrose,* which opens with the line: "Like one speaks to the stone, like/you,/to me from the abyss." The poem, as Werner Hamacher says, "describes the figure of an impossible dialogue."[20] The you and the I of the poem are caught in an unending, indeterminable interchange; they change places, inverting the direction of speaking, so that Hamacher can conclude:

> The irreconcilable ambiguity of Celan's formulation — in which the absence of the you suspends the I, that of the I suspends the you, and along with it discourse itself is suspended — realizes on the level of composition what the apostrophe says of the you[,] . . . that it is what

20. Werner Hamacher, "The Second of Inversion: Movements of a Figure through Celan's Poetry," *Yale French Studies* 69 (1985): 276–314, 294.

is "in the nothing of a night . . . encountered.". . . . As one speaks to the stone, so speaks the stone: to nobody and nothing.[21]

"The poem," Hamacher goes on, "is a texture of interrupted illocutionary acts and muteness, thus becomes itself the mute discourse of a stone, a nothing encountered." This most radically stated impossibility of speaking — and thus of witnessing — is linked in the third stanza to the murdered *Geschlecht* (a word that carries a constellation of meanings: sex, gender, race, generation, family, lineage, species, genre): "Who/who was it, that/lineage, the murdered one, the one/ standing black in the sky:/Rod and ball — ?" Celan answers this question in the following stanza — though he puts the answer in parentheses, indicating that this is somehow extraneous matter, finally not central to the poem, and yet it is there, stands centrally in the poem, this matter of, if I may permit myself to pun on the typographical symbol used by Celan, the *parent thesis:* "(Root./Root of Abraham. Root of Jesse. No one's/root — o/ours.)"

The root of the Jews, Abraham's, Jesse's, is also, now, after the Shoah, "no one's root." That "no one," that *Niemand,* already given in the title of the volume in which the poem appears as "Die Niemandsrose" and encountered in many versions throughout Celan's work, is no longer simply the figure of a straight inversion: that is, it does not simply mean the absence of someone. Hamacher, again:

> In this most radical version of inversion, language no longer converts
> its own nothingness into the substantial being of appearance, sound,
> and consciousness, as with Hegel and Rilke. Rather, it converts its
> literary being, compositionally and semantically, into nothing. This

21. Ibid., 295–96.

inversion is grounded in the third stanza's questioning after the murdered race.[22]

So here, in late Celan, the language itself in stating, imparting, acting the impossibility of speaking, becomes the very "stigma of the murder of European Jewry in the extermination camps of the Nazi regime." Peter Szondi countered Adorno's well-known dictum by saying, "After Auschwitz no poem is any longer possible except on the basis of Auschwitz." "Radix, Matrix" speaks out of that ground, but that ground, "Grund," has become an abyss, "Abgrund." Hamacher:

> [This abyss] is not the condition of its possibility but rather that of its impossibility. . . . [T]he poem is still only capable of speaking because it exposes itself to the impossibility of its speaking. It no longer speaks the language of a race that could be the ground, center, origin, father and mother. Rather it speaks — uprooted, orphaned — the language of the murdered. On this account Auschwitz, a name for innumerable unnamables, can never become for it a historically bound fact. Murder cannot become the univocal object of its speaking; it can only be the projection of a questioning that recognizes itself as objectless and mute, and therein as itself a victim of the murder.[23]

This is not the place to enter into a detailed analysis of this question of inversion. Suffice it to say that Celan's "Niemand" is clearly not a simple negative, the negation of a "someone." Rather it is the possibility of the impossibility of the poem itself, and that possibility of the impossibility of the poem is the only possibility that Celan will grant the poem after Auschwitz. It is from this no-place, this abyss, that the

22. Ibid., 296.
23. Ibid., 297.

poem speaks. It is that "Niemand" who does the witnessing in the verse: "Niemand zeugt für den Zeugen." Nobody witnesses for the witness. The impossible/possible poem witnesses for the witness. What Celan — as a "survivor," that is, as someone who should be dead, because he comes/is there after death, as someone whose life is in suspension, is a mere supplement of death — bears witness to, is another, a new way of speaking, the only way possible after the Shoah.

But this problematic of the witness has a further dimension, or, better, further dimensions, that I would like to explore here in some detail as one example of the complex polysemy that orchestrates so much of Celan's work, making its translation such an arduous task — with translation first of all being the most demanding and active reading to which we can submit ourselves and the poem. I first encountered these other layers of embedded meanings when attempting to translate the poem "Aschenglorie hinter" from the volume *Atemwende/Breathturn*.

This book is the first book after what is called Celan's "Wende," or turn, which I have elsewhere described as follows: "The poems, which had always been highly complex but rather lush with an abundance of near-surrealistic imagery & sometimes labyrinthine metaphoricity . . . were pared down, the syntax grew tighter & more spiny, his trademark neologisms & telescoping of words increased, while the overall composition of the work became much more 'serial' in nature, i.e. rather than insisting on individual, titled poems, he moved towards a method of composition by cycles & volumes."[24] This "turn" had been prepared for some years and can already be seen at work in the differences between the poetics of "Death Fugue" and those of "Stretto," as discussed above, though they become more radical, not to say ab-

24. See the introduction to *Breathturn*.

solute, from *Breathturn* onward (the title itself speaks of the "turn"). Already in 1958 Celan had suggested that for him poetry was no longer (if it had ever been) a matter of "transfiguring" *(verklären)*. He wrote that given the "sinister events in its memory," the language of German poetry has to become "more sober, more factual[,] ... 'grayer.'" This greater factuality checks a core impulse of the lyrical tradition, its relation to the "lyre," to music: "it is ... a language which wants to locate even its 'musicality' in such a way that it has nothing in common with the 'euphony' which more or less blithely continued to sound alongside the greatest horrors." The direct effect of giving up this "euphony" is to increase the accuracy of the language: "It does not transfigure or render 'poetical'; it names, it posits, it tries to measure the area of the given and the possible."[25]

Let us return now to "Aschenglorie hinter." The final stanza of the poem reads

Niemand
zeugt für den
Zeugen.

When I first ventured to translate the poem, this sentence seemed semantically unambiguous and the stanza easily became

Nobody
witnesses for the
witness.

At the time this formulation seemed both straightforward and extremely pregnant to me, encapsulating a central concern in Celan's work, namely, the concern that this tragedy would eventually, already

25. Celan, *Collected Prose*, 15–16.

in the second post-Shoah generation, become lost — not necessarily lost as a simple "forgetting," but lost into mere storytelling, "mythos," mythified, though made even more complex by a radical questioning of the very possibility of witnessing.

Moving deeper into Celan's work, reworking the translations of *Breathturn* and starting to translate later volumes, it became clear that the *zeugen/Zeuge* complex was much more semantically multilayered than I had at first perceived. The German word *zeugen* also has the meaning "to beget, to generate," a meaning kept more or less alive in the English word *testify* via its Latin root *testis,* which refers both to the "witness" and to "testicle" (as the "witness" of virility). One also has to keep in mind the "Rod and ball," the "Hode" from the poem "Radix, Matrix." (Another semantic extension would lead us to "testament," "testamentary" — clearly terms that can also play into the witness complex.) Unhappily, in English there is no synonym for *witness* based on the verb *to testify* (the back-formation *testifier* sounds odd and is unusable), and rendering the line as "nobody testifies for the witness," though getting in some of the semantic richness of the "zeugen" complex, ruins the poetics of the line and its use of repetition and internal rhyme, one of Celan's favorite and most pregnant technical devices. The most satisfactory solution I have (so far) found that takes the polysemy into consideration is the following version: "Noone/bears witness for the/witness," as an attentive reader can (one hopes) hear in the expression "to bear" some of the load of procreation that the German word carries.

More recently I have come across an excellent essay (which I recommend for any in-depth reading of this poem) by Jacques Derrida, who teases a further layer out of the Latin root *testis* by linking it to the word *terstis.* He quotes Emile Benveniste's *Dictionary of European Institutions:* "Etymologically, *testis* is someone who is present as a 'third' *(terstis)* at a transaction where two people are concerned." This linkage, so argues Derrida, will then also throw light on another obscure image in the poem, namely, the "Dreiweg," the "threeway" that occurs twice elsewhere in the poem. He writes: "The poem bears witness. We don't know about what and for what, about whom and for whom, in bearing witness for bearing witness, it bears witness. But it bears witness. As a result, what it says of the witness it also says of itself as witness or as witnessing. As poetic witnessing."[26]

But beyond the witnessing to the past, Celan also witnesses for the possibility of a *vita nuova,* a new life — maybe only or mainly in an indirect way, that is, by bearing witness (as Derrida points out) to the possibility of the poem and by having the poem itself say that witnessing. A poem from *Breathturn,* a poem whose importance is signaled by the fact that one of its composita will become the title of the next volume, *Threadsuns,* reads

> threadsuns
> Above the grayblack wastes.
> A tree-
> high thought
> grasps the light-tone: there are
> still songs to sing beyond
> mankind.

As I wrote of this poem in the introduction to that volume, "These 'Fadensonnen,' these threadsuns fold into the word that gives their elongation — the 'Faden,' the thread — something more, something which in English is still there in the word 'fathom,' which comes to us

26. Jacques Derrida, "'A Self-Unsealing Poetic Text': Poetics and Politics of Witnessing," in *Revenge of the Aesthetic: The Place of Literature in Theory Today,* edited by Michael P. Clark (Berkeley: University of California Press, 2000), 186, 198.

via the Indo-European root *pet* and Germanic *fathmaz:* 'the length of two arms stretched out.'" The thread is thus a way of measuring space, or of "sounding" depth (the poem also speaks of a "Lichtton," a "light-tone" or sound) and, maybe, of a measure, or a new measure for the world and for poetry. If the first volume that announced the late work and its radically innovative poetics had been called *Breathturn,* to indicate that a turn, a change, was needed — had in fact taken place — then the title of this, the next volume, spoke of a new measure, of new measures, to be accurate. Of those new measures needed in a world seen as "grayblack wastes" to link the above and the below, the inside and the outside, the tree-high thought and the wastes, because, Celan goes on, "there still are/songs to be sung," poems to be written even under the duress — *Lightduress* will be the title of the next collection — of the present condition. Even if these poems are "beyond mankind" — beyond any older humanistic category of aesthetics. (As he told Esther Cameron at this time: "But I don't give a damn for aesthetic construction.") His writing had moved toward such a post-aesthetic, posthumanist condition nearly from the start, even if early work, say, the "Todesfuge," achieves this only through an acidly sarcastic use of a traditional aesthetic form. It was the late work that would realize this condition, exactly. Or, as Hugo Huppert remembers Celan's words:

> I don't musicalize anymore, as at the time of the much-touted "Todesfuge," which by now has been threshed over in many a textbook. . . . As for my alleged encodings, I'd rather say: Polysemy without mask, thus corresponding exactly to my sense of the intersection of ideas *(Begriffsüberschneidung),* the overlapping of relations. You are aware of the phenomenon of interference, the effect of waves of the same frequency coming together. . . . I try to reproduce cuttings from the spectral analysis of things, to show them in several aspects

and permeations at once. . . . I see my alleged abstractness and actual ambiguity as moments of realism.[27]

On April 6, 1970, Paul Celan wrote in a letter to his friend Ilana Shmueli: "When I read my poems, they grant me, momentarily, the possibility to exist, to stand."[28] Two weeks later Celan gave himself over to the drift of the Seine, exhausted after having stood tirelessly, selflessly for the possibility of a new life. His is the life of the survivor, yes, but not only: it is essential today, I believe, to give Paul Celan back the spread of *humanitas* he wanted and stood for with his life and work, with the *Dichtung* and the *Wahrheit* of the life and work. We are only beginning to learn how to read Paul Celan's work, and maybe the best way to approach this task is to take to heart what he said in an unsent letter to René Char (p. 184): "To that in your work which did not — or not yet — open up to my comprehension, I responded with respect and by waiting: one can never pretend to comprehend completely — : that would be disrespect in the face of the Unknown that inhabits — or comes to inhabit — the poet; that would be to forget that poetry is something one breathes; that poetry breathes you in."

27. Werner Hamacher and Winfried Menninghaus, eds., *Paul Celan* (Frankfurt am Main: Suhrkamp Verlag, 1988), 320–21.

28. Ilana Schmueli, *Sag, dass Jerusalem ist. Über Paul Celan: Oktober 1969–April 1970* (Eggingen: Edition Isele, 2000), 75.

KEY TO TRANSLATORS

NC *Norma Cole*

CC *Cid Corman*

PJ *Pierre Joris*

RK *Robert Kelly*

JN *Joachim Neugroschel*

JR *Jerome Rothenberg*

RW *Rosmarie Waldrop*

Previous page:
Gisèle Celan-Lestrange,
etching, no. 4 in the series
Atemkristall.

from ROMANIAN PROSE POEMS

AS PARTISAN OF EROTIC ABSOLUTISM, reticent megalomaniac even among divers, and simultaneous messenger of Paul Celan's halo, I evoke the petrified apparitions of the sunk airship only every ten (or more) years, and I go skating only at the latest hour on a lake guarded by the giant forest of brainless members of the world-poets-conspiracy. It's easy to understand that here you cannot get through with the arrows of visible fire. At the border of the world an infinitely large amethyst-curtain hides the existence of that human-shaped vegetation beyond which I, selenic, attempt a dance supposed to make me ecstatic. But so far I have not succeeded, and with my eyes, which have migrated to my temples, I contemplate my profile, waiting for spring.

• PJ •

THE SAND FROM THE URNS

Moldgreen is the house of forgetting.
Before each of the blowing gates your decapitated bandsman blues.
For you he beats the drum of moss and bitter pubic hair;
with festering toe he draws your brow in the sand.
He draws it longer than it was, and the red of your lip.
You fill the urns here and feed your heart.

• PJ •

IN PRAISE OF REMOTENESS

In the wellspring of your eyes
live the fish-nets of the labyrinth-sea.
In the wellspring of your eyes
the ocean keeps its promise.

Here I, a
heart that lingered among men,
cast off my clothes and the luster of a vow:

Blacker in black, I am nuder.
Only when faithless am I true.
I am you when I am I.

In the wellspring of your eyes
I drift and dream about prey.

A net snared a net:
we separate entwined.

In the wellspring of your eyes
a hanged man strangles the rope.

• JN •

CORONA

Autumn is eating a leaf from my hand: we are friends.
We are picking time out of a nut, we teach it to run:
and time rushes back to its shell.

In the mirror it's Sunday,
in dreams people sleep,
the mouth tells the truth.

My eye descends to the sex of my loved one,
we gaze at each other,
we whisper out darkness,
we love one another like poppies and memory,
we sleep like wine in a seashell,
like the sea in the moon's bloody rays.

Embracing we stand by the window, and people look up from
    the street:
it is time that they knew!
It is time that the stone grew accustomed to blooming,

that unrest formed a heart.
It is time it was time.

It is time.

· JR ·

DEATH FUGUE

Black milk of morning we drink you at dusktime
we drink you at noontime and dawntime we drink you at night
we drink and drink
we scoop out a grave in the sky where it's roomy to lie
There's a man in this house who cultivates snakes and who writes
who writes when it's nightfall *nach Deutschland* your golden hair
   Margareta
he writes it and walks from the house and the stars all start flashing
   he whistles his dogs to draw near
whistles his Jews to appear starts us scooping a grave out of sand
he commands us play up for the dance

Black milk of morning we drink you at night
we drink you at dawntime and noontime we drink you at dusktime
we drink and drink
There's a man in this house who cultivates snakes and who writes
who writes when it's nightfall *nach Deutschland* your golden hair
   Margareta
your ashen hair Shulamite we scoop out a grave in the sky where it's
   roomy to lie

He calls jab it deep in the soil you men you other men sing and play
he tugs at the sword in his belt he swings it his eyes are blue
jab your spades deeper you men you other men play up again for
  the dance

Black milk of morning we drink you at night
we drink you at noontime and dawntime we drink you at dusktime
we drink and drink
there's a man in this house your golden hair Margareta
your ashen hair Shulamite he cultivates snakes

He calls play that death thing more sweetly Death is a gang-boss
  aus Deutschland
he calls scrape that fiddle more darkly then hover like smoke in
  the air
then scoop out a grave in the clouds where it's roomy to lie

Black milk of morning we drink you at night
we drink you at noontime Death is a gang-boss *aus Deutschland*
we drink you at dusktime and dawntime we drink and drink
Death is a gang-boss *aus Deutschland* his eye is blue
he hits you with leaden bullets his aim is true
there's a man in this house your golden hair Margareta
he sets his dogs on our trail he gives us a grave in the sky
he cultivates snakes and he dreams Death is a gang-boss *aus
  Deutschland*

your golden hair Margareta
your ashen hair Shulamite

· JR ·

THE JARS

for Klaus Demus

At the long tables of time
God's jars are boozing.
They guzzle the eyes of the seeing and the eyes of the blind,
the hearts of the ruling shadows,
the hollow cheek of evening.
They are the mightiest boozers:
they raise to their lips the empty as well as the full
and don't spill over like you or I.

• P J •

COUNT the almonds,
count what was bitter and kept you awake,
count me in with them:

I searched for your eye which you opened when nobody saw you,
I spun that mysterious thread
down which the dew that you dreamed
slithered into a pitcher
kept from harm by a word found in nobody's heart.

There you first came into a name that was yours,
sure of foot you advanced on yourself,
the clappers swung free in your silence's belltower,
whatever you heard took a hold of you,
whatever was dead laid its hand on you too,
and threefold you moved through the evening.

Make me bitter.
Count me in with the almonds.

· JR ·

from VON SCHWELLE ZU SCHWELLE /
FROM THRESHOLD TO THRESHOLD

I HEARD IT SAID

I heard it said there was
a stone in the water and a circle,
and above the water a word
that lays the circle around the stone.

I saw my poplar go down to the water,
I saw her arm reach down into the depth,
I saw her roots beg skyward for night.

I did not run after her,
I only picked up from the ground the crumb
that has your eye's shape and nobility,
I took the chain of proverbs off your neck
and with it hemmed the table where the crumb now lay.

And no longer saw my poplar.

• PJ •

WITH A VARIABLE KEY

With a variable key
you unlock the house, in it
drifts the snow of the unsaid.
Depending on the blood that gushes
from your eye or mouth or ear,
your key varies.

Varies your key so varies your word
that's allowed to drift with the flakes.
Depending on the wind that pushes you away,
the snow cakes around the word.

· P J ·

SHIBBOLETH

Along with my stone
like a great tear that fell
in back of the shutters,

they hauled me
into the dust of a market,
that place
where a flag was unrolled
to which I never had sworn.

Flutes,
double-flutes of the night:
remember the dark
and twin redness,
Madrid and Vienna.

Memory,
set up your flag at half-mast.
At half-mast
today and forever.

Heart:
let us see you here too,

here in the dust of this market.
Thunder your shibboleth here
into your alien homeland:
February. *No pasarán.*

Unicorn:
you know of the stones
you know of the water,
come,
let me lead you away
toward the voices
of Estremadura.

· JR ·

SPEAK, YOU TOO

Speak, you too,
speak as the last one,
have your say.

Speak —
But do not separate the no from the yes.
Give your saying also meaning:
give it its shadow.

Give it enough shadow,
give it as much
as you know to be parceled out between
midnight and midday and midnight.

Look around:
see how alive it gets all around —
At death! Alive!
Speaks true, who speaks shadows.

But now the place shrinks, on which you stand:
Whereto now, shadow-stripped one, whereto?
Climb. Feel yourself upwards.
Thinner you become, unrecognizable, finer!

Finer: a fathom
along which it wants to descend, the star:
to swim down below, below
where he sees himself swimming: in the swell
of wandering words.

· PJ ·

THE VINTAGERS

For Nani and Klaus Demus

They gather the grapes of their eyes,
they tread all weeping, even this:
the night wills it,
the night on which they are leaning, the wall,
the stone demands it,
the stone over which their cane speaks away
into the hush of the answer —
their cane that once,
once in autumn,
when the year swells towards death, as a cluster of grapes,
the cane that speaks once through the muteness, down
into the shaft of the imagined.

They gather, they tread the grapes,
they press time like their eye,
they cellar the seeping, the weeping,
in the sun's grave that they prepare
with a night-strong hand:
so that a mouth may thirst for it, later —

a late-mouth, akin to theirs:
bent towards blindness and paralyzed,
a mouth to which the draught foams up from the depth, while
the sky descends into the waxen sea
to glow from afar as a candle-stub
when the lip moistens at last.

· JN ·

Voices, in green of watersurface
sketched. When the kingfisher dives,
the second whizzes:

What stood by you
on either shore
it steps
mown into another scene.

■

Voices from the nettlepath:

Come on your hands to us. Who is alone with
the lamp has only his hand to read from.

■

Voices, nightpervaded, ropes on which
you hang the bell.

Arch over, world:
When the shell of death comes floating in, it will toll here.

■

Voices, at which your heart
back into your mother's heart shrinks.
Voices from the gallowstree,
where slowwood and quickwood exchange
and exchange rings.

■

Voices, fullthroated, in slag, where even the
Infinite shovels, (hearr-) slimy runnel.

Set the boats out here, child, which I
manned:

When midships the squall takes command, the bolts
strain together.

■

Jacobsvoice:

The tears.
The tears in brothereye.
One left hanging, grew.
We dwell there.
Breathe, that
it let go.

■

Voices from within the ark:

It is
only the mouths are saved. You
who go down, hear us too.

■

No
voice — a
slowsound, timestrange, to your
thoughts bestowed, here, at last
hereawakens: a
fruitleaf, eyesized, deep
scratched; it
oozes, will not
scab over.

• CC •

TENEBRAE

Nigh are we, Lord,
near and graspable.

Gripped already, Lord,
in each other clutched, as though
the body of each of us were
your body, Lord.

Pray, Lord,
Pray to us,
we are nigh.

Windskew we went on,
we went on, to bend ourselves
at hollow and hole.

To the trough we went, Lord.

It was blood, it was,
which you had spilt, Lord.

It glittered.

It cast your image into our eyes, Lord.
Eyes and mouth hang so open and empty, Lord.
We *have* drunk, Lord.
The blood and the image within the blood, Lord.

Pray, Lord.
We are nigh.

• CC •

SPEECH-GRILLE

Eye-orb between the bars.

Ciliary lid
rows upwards,
releases a gaze.

Iris, swimmer, dreamless and dim:
the sky, heart-gray, must be near.

Skew, in the iron socket,
the smoldering splinter.
By the sense of light
you guess the soul.

(Were I like you. Were you like me.
Did we not stand
under *one* tradewind
We are strangers.)

The tiles. Upon them,
close together, the two

heart-gray pools:
two
mouthfuls of silence.

• JN •

MATIÈRE DE BRETAGNE

Furze-light, yellow, the slopes
fester skywards, the thorn
woos the wound, a knell tolls
within, it is evening, the void
rolls its seas to devotion,
the blood-sail steers at you.

Arid, aground,
the bed behind you, sedge-choked
its hour, above,
at the star, the milky
narrows chatter in mud, stone-borer,
below, bushy, gapes into blueness, a shrub of
ephemeralness, lovely,
hails your memory.

(Did you know me,   .
hands? I followed
the forking road you showed me, my mouth
spit out its chippings, I walked, my time,
ja wandering snow-wall, cast its shadow — did you know me?)

Hands, the thorn-
wooed wound, a knell,
hands, the void, its seas,
hands, in the furze-light, the
blood-sail
steers at you.

You
you teach
you teach your hands
you teach your hands you teach
you teach your hands
to sleep

• JN •

STRETTO

■

Spent into
the ground
with unmistakable trace:

grass, written asunder. The stones, white,
with the shadows of the stalks:
Stop reading: look!
Stop looking: go!

Go, your hour
has no sisters, you are —
are at home. A wheel, slowly,
rolls by itself, the spokes
clamber,
clamber over the darkening field, night
needs no stars, nothing
is asking about you.

■

                              Nothing
                              asking about you —

The place, where they lay, it has
a name — it has
none. They didn't lie there. Something
lay between them. They
didn't see through it.

Didn't see, no,
spoke about
words. Nothing
woke up,
sleep
came over them.

■

                                Came, came. Nothing
                                       asking —

It's me, me,
I lay between you, I was
open, was
audible, I ticked to you, your breath
obeyed, I
am still the one, you
still are sleeping.

■

                                   Am still the one —

Years.
Years, years, a finger
feels down and up, feels

around:
where the seams are, feel them, here
it ripped wide apart, here
it grew back together — who
covered it up?

■

                                    Covered it
                                    up — who?

Came, came.
Came a word, came,
came through the night,
wanted to shine, wanted to shine.

Ashes.
Ashes, ashes.
Night.
Night-and-night. — To
the eye, go, to the moist.

■

                 To

                       the eye, go,

                                    to the moist —

hurricanes,
hurricanes, from wherever,
particle drift, the other,
you

know the one, we
read it in the book, it was
meaning.

Was, was
meaning. How
did we grasp
each other — with
these
hands?

And it stood written that.
Where? We
did a silence over it,
venomstilled, huge,
a
green
silence, a sepal, a
thought of plant life hung from it —
green, yes,
hung, yes,
under spiteful
skies.

Of, yes,
plant life.

Yes.
Hurricanes, par-
ticle drift, some
time left, left,

to try it on the stone — it
was hospitable, it
didn't interrupt. How
good we had it:

gritty,
gritty and stringy. Stalked,
dense;
clustery and raying; kidneyshaped,
flattish and
lumpy; loose, all
branching, it, it
didn't interrupt, it
spoke,
spoke gladly to dry eyes before it closed them.

Spoke, spoke.
Was, was.

We
did not give way, stood
in the midst,
pore structure, and
it came.

Came up to us, came
right through, stitched
invisibly, stitched
to the last membrane,
and
the world, a thousand crystal,
shot forth, shot forth.

∎

                              Shot forth, shot forth.
                                        Then —

nights, unmixed, circles,
green or blue, red
squares: the
world puts its innermost
into play with the new
hours. — Circles,
red or black, bright
squares, no
flight shadows,
no
measuring board, no
smoke soul rises and plays too.

∎

                              Rises and
                                   plays too —

In owl flight, near
leprosy turned to stone,
near
our fled hands, in
the latest rejection,
over the
target on
the ruinous wall:

visible, once
again: the
furrows, the

choirs, back then, the
psalms. Ho, ho
sanna.

So
temples still stand. A
star
still has its light.
Nothing,
nothing is lost.

Ho-
sanna.

In the owl flight, here,
the chatter, day gray,
of groundwater traces.

■

        (— day gray,
    of
            groundwater traces —

Spent
into the ground
with

the unmistakable
trace:

grass.
Grass,
written asunder.)

• RK •

from DIE NIEMANDSROSE /
THE NOONESROSE

THERE WAS EARTH IN THEM, and they dug.

They dug and dug, so passed
their day away, their night. And they praised not God,
who, as they heard, wished all this,
who, as they heard, knew all this.

They dug and heard no more;
they became not wise, made up no song, devised no kind of tongue
for themselves. They dug.

There came a stillness, and there came a storm, there came the
oceans all. I dig, you dig, and so too digs the worm, and the
singing there means: They dig.

O one, O none, O nobody, you:
Where to go, with nowhere to go?
O you dig and I dig, and I dig unto you,
and a-finger awakens us the ring.

• CC •

ZÜRICH, ZUM STORCHEN

for Nelly Sachs

Of too much was the talk, of
too little. Of you
and again-you, of
the dimming through brightness, of
Jewishness, of
your God.

Thereof.
The day of an Ascension, the cathedral stood
off there, came with something of gold over
the water.

Of your God was the talk, I spoke
against him, I
let the heart that I had
hope:
for
its highest, deathrattled, its
cavilling word —

Your eye looked at me, looked away,
your mouth
addressed the eye, I heard:

We
dont (really) know, you know(?),
we
dont (really) know,
what's
worth.

· CC ·

PSALM

Noone kneads us again from earth and loam,
noone evokes our dust.
Noone.

Praised be you, noone.
Because of you we wish
to bloom.
Against
you.

A nothing
were we, are we, will
we be, blossoming:
the nothing's-, the noonesrose.

With
its pistil soulbright,
its stamen heavencrazed,
its crown red
from the purpleword that we sang
over, o over
its thorn.

· CC ·

TÜBINGEN, JÄNNER

Eyes con-
vinced to go blind.
Their — "a
riddle is pure
origin" — , their
remembrance of
swimming Hölderlin-towers, gull-
blown.

Visits of drowned carpenters by
these
diving words:

If,
if a man,
if a man was born, today, with
the lightbeard of
the patriarchs: he could,
speaking of these
days, he
could
but babble and babble.

always, always
agagain.

("Pallaksch. Pallaksch.")

· PJ ·

ALCHEMICAL

Silence, cooked like gold, in
carbonized
hands.

Great, gray,
close, like all that's lost,
sister figure:

All the Names, all the al-
names. So much
to be blessed ashes. So much
won land
above
the light, o so light
soul-
rings.

Great. Gray. Cinder-
less.

You. Back then.
You with the livid

bitten open bud.
You in the wine-flood.

(Isn't it true, us too
this clock released?
Good,
good, how your word died past here.)

Silence, cooked like gold, in
carbonized, carbonized
hands.
Finger, smoke-thin. Like crowns, aircrowns
around —

Great. Gray. Trace-
less.
King-
ly.

· PJ ·

RADIX, MATRIX

Like one speaks to the stone, like
you,
to me from the abyss, from
a homeland hereward, dis-
sister, hereward
thrown one, you,
you pretime for me,
you me in the nothing of a night,
you in the but-night en-
countered one, you
but-you — :

Back when, when I was not there,
back when, when you
paced off the field, alone:

Who,
who was it, that
lineage, the murdered one, the one
standing black into the sky:
Rod and ball — ?

(Root.
Root of Abraham. Root of Jesse. No one's
root — oh
ours.)

Yes,
as one speaks to the stone, as
you
with my hands thereto
and into nothingness grab, thus
is, what is here:

this receptacle
too gapes,
this
downward
is the one of the wild-
blooming crowns.

· P J ·

BLACKEARTH. black
earth you, times-
mother
Despair:

One from the hand and its
wound to you De-
livered shuts
your calyxes.

         • CC •

TO ONE WHO STOOD AT THE DOOR, one
evening:

to him
I let my word out — : to the
goitred I saw him trot, to the
half-
hearted, the
muddy booted footsoldier
born brother, the
blood-glutted
Gods-
handiwork, the
chittering little man.

Rabbi, I rasped, Rabbi
Loew:

From him
remove the word,
for him
write the living
nothingness at heart,
to him
extend your two

brokenfingers in grace-
bestowing judgment.
To him.

. . . .

Throw eveningsdoor open too, Rabbi.

. . . .

Rip the morningsdoor off, Ra⁻—

• CC •

MANDORLA

In the almond — what stands in the almond?
Nothing.
What stands in the almond is Nothing.
There it stands and stands.

In Nothing — what stands there? The King.
There the King stands, the King.
There he stands and stands.

   Jew's curl, you'll not turn gray.

And your eye — what does your eye stand on?
On the almond your eye stands.
Your eye, on Nothing it stands.
Stands on the King, to him remains loyal, true.
So it stands and stands.

   Human curl, you'll not turn gray.
   Empty almond, royal-blue.

· PJ ·

SIBERIAN

Bowprayers — you
didn't recite them along, they were,
you think so, yours.

The crow-swan hung
from the early asterism:
with corroded lid fissure
a face stood — even under this
shadow.

Small bell, left
lying in the
icewind
with your
white pebble in the mouth:

Stuck in my
throat too, the millennium-
colored stone, the heartstone,
I too

develop verdigris on
my lip.

Over the rubble field here,
through the sedge sea today
she leads, our
bronze-road.
There I lie and talk to you
with skinned
finger.

• PJ •

THE SYLLABLE PAIN

It gave itself into Your hand:
a You, deathless,
at which all of I came to itself. Wordfree
voices drove around, empty forms, everything
entered them, mixed
and unmixed
and mixed
again.

And numbers too
were woven into the
uncountable. One and a thousand and what
before and after
was larger than itself, smaller, ripe-
ned and
back- and out-
transformed into
germinating Never.

The forgotten groped
the to-be-forgotten, continents, heartinents
swam,

sank and swam. Columbus,
fall
crocus in his sight, the mother-
flower,
murdered masts and sails. Everything left port,

free,
explorerish,
the windrose flowered and faded, ex-
foliated, a worldsea
bloomed a-heap and a-day, in the blacklight
of wild-lubber lines. In coffins,
urns, canopic jars
the little children
awoke : Jasper, Agate, Amethyst — peoples,
tribes and clans, a blind

L e t   t h e r e   b e

knotted itself in-
to the serpentheaded free-
ropes — : a
knot
(and counter- and contra- and yet- and twin- and thou-
sandknot), which
the carnival-sucking brood
of martenstars in the abyss
spell-, spell-, spelled
out, out.

· PJ ·

AND WITH THE BOOK FROM TARUSSA

All poets are Jews
— *Marina Tsvetayeva*

Of the
constellation of Canis, of the
bright-star in it and the dwarf-
light that also weaves
on roads mirrored earthwards,

of
pilgrim-staffs, there too, of the south, alien
and nightfiber-near
like unsepulchered words,
roaming
in the orbit of attained
goals and stelae and cradles.

Of things
sooth-said and fore-told and spoken over to you,
of things

talked upwards,
on the alert, akin to one
of one's own heart-stones, that one spewed out
together with their in-
destructible clockwork, out
into unland and untime. Of such
ticking and ticking amid
the gravel-cubes with
(going back on a hyena spoor
traceable upwards)
the ancestral
line of Those-
of-the-Name-and-Its-
Round-Abyss.

Of
a tree, of one.
Yes, of it too. And of the woods around it. Of the woods
Untrodden, of the
thought they grew from, as sound
and half-sound and changed sound and terminal sound, Scythian
rhymes
in the meter
of the temple and of the driven,
with
breathed steppe-
grass written into the heart
of the hour-caesuras — into the realm,

the widest of
realms, into
the great internal rhyme
beyond
the zone of mute nations, into yourself
language-scale, word-scale, home-
scale of exile.

Of this tree, these woods.

Of the bridge's
broadstone, from which
he bounced across into
life, full-fledged
by wounds — of the
Pont Mirabeau.
Where the Oka doesn't flow. Et quels
amours! (Cyrillic, friends, I rode
this too across the Seine,
rode it across the Rhine.)

Of a letter, of it.
Of the one-letter, East-letter. Of the hard and
tiny word-heap, of the
unarmed eye that it
transmits to
the three
belt-stars of Orion — Jacob's
staff, you,
once again you come walking! —

on the
celestial chart that opened for it.

Of the table where this happened.

Of a word, from the heap
on which it, the table
became a galley-seat, from the Oka River
and its waters.

Of the passing word that
    a galley-slave gnash-echos, into the late-summer reeds
of his keen-
eared thole-pin:

Colchis.

· JN ·

YOU MAY confidently
regale me with snow:
as often as I strode through summer
shoulder to shoulder with the mulberry tree,
its youngest leaf
shrieked.

IN THE RIVERS north of the future
I cast the net, which you
hesitantly weight
with shadows stones
wrote.

TO STAND, in the shadow
of the stigma in the air.
Standing-for-no-one-and-nothing.

Unrecognized,
for you
alone.

With all that has room in it,
even without
language.

THREADSUNS
above the grayblack wastes.
A tree-
high thought
grasps the light-tone: there are
still songs to sing beyond
mankind.

WORDACCRETION, volcanic,
drowned out by searoar.

Above,
the flooding mob
of the contra-creatures: it
flew a flag — portrait and replica
cruise vainly timeward.

Till you hurl forth the word-
moon, out of which

the wonder ebb occurs
and the heart-
shaped crater
testifies naked for the beginnings,
the kings-
births.

SINGABLE REMNANT — the outline
of him, who through
the sicklescript broke through unvoiced,
apart, at the snowplace.

Whirling
under comet-
brows
the gaze's bulk, towards
which the eclipsed, tiny
heart-satellite drifts
with the
spark caught outside.

— Disenfranchised lip, announce,
that something happens, still,
not far from you.

NO SANDART ANYMORE, no sandbook, no masters.

Nothing in the dice. How
many mutes?
Seventen.

Your question — your answer.
Your chant, what does it know?

Deepinsnow,
        Eepinno,
                I-i-o.

HARBOR

Sorehealed: where-,
when you were like me, criss-
and crossdreamt by
schnappsbottlenecks at the
whore table

— cast
my happiness aright, Seahair,
heap up the wave, that carries me, Blackcurse,
break your way
through the hottest womb,
Icesorrowpen — ,

where-
to
didn't you come to lie with me, even

on the benches
at Mother Clausen's, yes, she
knows, how often I sang all
the way up into your throat, hey-diddle-doo,
like the bilberryblue
alder of homeland with all its leaves,
hey-doodle-dee,
you, like the
astral-flute from
beyond the worldridge — there too
we swam, nakednudes, swam,
the abyssverse on
the fire red forehead — unconsumed by
fire the deep-
inside flooding gold
dug its paths upwards —,

                                    here,
with eyelashed sails,
remembrance too drove past, slowly
the conflagration jumped over, cut-
off, you,
cut off on
the two blue-
black memory-
barges,
but driven on now also
by the thousand-
arm, with which I held you,
they cruise, past starthrow-dives,

our still drunk, still drinking
byworldly mouths — I name only them —

till over there at the timegreen clocktower
the net-, the numberskin soundlessly
peels off — a delusion-dock,
swimming, before it,
off-world-white the
letters of the
cat, the trolley, life, which
the sense-
greedy sentences dredge up, after midnight,
at which
neptunic sin throws its corn-
schnapps-colored towrope,
between
twelve-
toned lovesoundbuoys
— draw-well-winch back then, with you
it sings in the no longer
inland choir —
the beaconlightships come dancing,
from afar, from Odessa,

the loadline,
which sinks with us, true to our burden,
Owlglasses all that
downwards, upwards, and why not? *sorehealed, where-,*
when-
hither and past and hither.

THE JUGGLERDRUM,
from my heartpenny loud.

The rungs of the ladder, up
which Ulysses, my monkey, clambers toward Ithaca,
rue de Longchamp, one hour
after the spilled wine:

add that to the image,
which casts us home into
the dice-cup, where I lie by you,
unplayable.

IN PRAGUE

Half-death,
suckled on our life,
lay ash-image-true around us —

we too
kept on drinking, soul-crossed, two swords,
stitched to heavenstones, born of wordblood,
in the nightbed,

larger and larger
we grew, intergrafted, there was
no name left for
what urged us on (one of thirty-
-and-how-many

was my living shadow,
who climbed up the delusion-stairs to you?)

a tower,
the half-one built into the Whither,
a Hradshin
all of goldmaker's No,

bone-Hebrew,
ground to sperm,
ran through the hourglass,
through which we swam, two dreams now, tolling
against time, on the squares.

ASHGLORY behind
your shaken-knotted
hands at the threeway.

Pontic erstwhile: here,
a drop,
on
the drowned rudder blade,
deep
in the petrified oath,
it roars up.

(On the vertical
breathrope, in those days,
higher than above,

between two painknots, while
the glossy
Tatarmoon climbed up to us,
I dug myself into you and into you.)

Ash-
glory behind
you threeway
hands.

The cast-in-front-of-you, from
the East, terrible.

Noone
bears witness for the
witness.

THE WRITTEN hollows itself, the
spoken, seagreen,
burns in the bays,

in the liquified names
the dolphins dart,

in the eternalized Nowhere, here,
in the memory of the over-
loud bells in — where only?

who
pants

in this
shadow-quadrat, who
from beneath it
shimmers, shimmers, shimmers?

FRIHED

In the house of the doubled delusion,
where the stoneboats fly
over
Whiteking's pier, toward the secrets,
where finally with
cut cord the
man-of-war-word cruises,

I, reed-pith nourished, am
in you, on
wild ducks' ponds,

I sing —

what do I sing?

The saboteur's
coat
with the red, the white
circles around the
bullet
holes
— through them

you sight the with us driving
free-
starry Above —
covers us, now,

the verdigris-nobility from the quay,
with its burned-brick thoughts
round about the forehead,
heaps the spirit round, the spindrift,

quick
the noises wither
this side and that side of mourning,

the crown's
closer-
sailing pus-prong
in the eye of one
born crooked
writes poems
in Danish.

SOLVE

De-easterned tomb-
tree, split into
firebrands:

past the Poison-
Palatinates, past the cathedrals,

upstream, down-
stream, rafted

by the tiny-flaring, by the
free
punctuation mark of the
script salvaged and dis-
solved into the count-
less to-be-
named un-
pronounceable
names.

COAGULA

Your wound
too, Rosa.

And the hornslight of your
Romanian buffaloes
in star's stead above the
sandbed, in the
talking, red-
ember-mighty
alembic.

ONCE
I did hear him,
he did wash the world,
unseen, nightlong,
real.

One and unending,
annihilated,
I'ed.

Light was. Salvation.

ALL POEMS IN THIS SECTION
TRANSLATED BY PIERRE JORIS

FRANKFURT, SEPTEMBER

Blind, light-
bearded partition.
A cockchaferdream
floodlights it.

Behind it, complaint-rastered,
Freud's forehead opens up,

the tear, hard-
silenced outside,
links on with the sentence:
"For the last
time psycho-
logy."

The imitation
jackdaw
breakfasts.

The glottal stop
sings.

DETOUR-
MAPS, phosphorous,
far behind Here by sheer
ring-fingers beaten.

Travelluck, look:

The tripdart, two
inches from the target,
topples
into the aorta.

The shared goods, ten
hundredweight
folie à deux,
wake up
in the vultureshadow,
in the seventeenth liver, at the foot
of the stuttering
information mast.

Before it,
in the slated watershield, the
three standing whales
head the ball.

A right eye
flashes.

SPASMS, I love you, psalms,

the feeling-walls deep in the you-ravine
rejoice, seedpainted one,

Eternal, de-eternalized are you
eternalized, Uneternal, you,

hey,

into you, into you
I sing the bone-rod-scratch,

Redred, far behind the pubic hair
harped, in the caves,

outside, all around
the unending none-whatsoever-canon,

you throw me the nine times
twined, dripping
eyetooth-wreath.

PAU, LATER

In the corner of
your eyes, stranger,
the albigenses-shadow —

after
the Waterloo-Plein,

towards the orphaned
raffia shoe, towards
the also bartered Amen,
into the eternal
housegap I
sing you:

so that Baruch, he who never
weeps,
may grind aright
all around you the
angular,
ununderstood, seeing
tear.

THE STALLION with the flowering wick,
levitating, at pass-
height,
comet brilliance on
the rump.

You, in the con-
spirationary torrents un-
locked, the
bouncing breasts in the sharp
verse-fibula-yoke,
fall with me through
images, rocks, numbers.

LYON, LES ARCHERS

The iron spike, reared,
in the brickniche:
the co-millennium,
instranges itself, unconquerable,
follows
your driving eyes,

now,
with glances cast here by dice
you wake, who is beside you,
she becomes heavier,
heavier,

you too, with all
the instrangedness in you,
instrange yourself,
deeper,

the One
string
tenses its pain between you,

the missing target
radiates, bow.

THE INDUSTRIOUS
mineral resources, homey,

the heated syncope,

the not-to-be-deciphered
jubilee,

the completely glassed in
spider-altars in the all-
overtowering low building,

the intermediate sounds
(even yet?)
the shadowpalavers,

the anxieties, icetrue,
flightclear,

the baroquely cloaked,
language-swallowing showerroom,
semantically floodlit,

the uninscribed wall
of a standing-cell:

here

live yourself
straightthrough, without clock.

WHEN I DON'T KNOW, DON'T KNOW,
without you, without you, without a You,

they all come,
the
freebeheaded, who
lifelong brainlessly sang
of the tribe
of the You-less:

Aschrej,

a word without meaning,
transtibetan,
injected into the
Jewess
Pallas
Athena's
helmeted ovaries,

and when he,

he,

fetally,

harps Carpathian notnot,

then the Allemande
bobbins her lace for

the vomiting im-
mortal
song.

YOU WERE my death:
you I could hold,
when all fell from me.

LINE THE WORDCAVES
with panther skins,

widen them, hide-to and hide-fro,
sense-hither and sense-thither,

give them courtyards, chambers, trapdoors
and wildnesses, parietal,

and listen for their second
and each time second and second
tone.

NEAR, IN THE AORTIC ARCH,
in the light-blood:
the light-word.

Mother Rachel
weeps no more.
Carried over:
all the weepings.

Quiet, in the coronary arteries,
unconstricted:
Ziv, that light.

IMAGINE

Imagine:
the moorsoldier from Masada
teaches himself homeland, in
the most inextinguishable way,
against
all barbs in the wire.

Imagine:
the eyeless without shape
lead you free through the throng, you
grow stronger and
stronger.

Imagine: your
own hand
has held once
more this
into life re-
suffered
piece of
inhabitable earth.

Imagine:
that came towards me,
awake to the name, awake to the hand,
forever,
from what cannot be buried.

ALL POEMS IN THIS SECTION
TRANSLATED BY PIERRE JORIS

SOUNDSCRAPS, VISIONSCRAPS, on
ward onethousandandone,

daynightly
the Bear-Polka:

they retrain you,

you again become
he.

WE ALREADY LAY
deep in the underbrush, when you
finally crept along.
But we could not
darken over towards you:
there reigned
lightduress.

CONTACT MINES on your left
moons, Saturn.

Shardsealed
the orbits out there.

Now must be the moment
for a just
birth.

CLEARED, this start
also.

Bow-wheelchant with
Corona.

The duskrudder responds,
your torn-
awake vein
unknots itself,

what's left of you, slants,
you gain
altitude.

ONCE, death was much in demand,
you hid in me.

TWO AT BRANCUSI'S

If one among these stones
were to tell
what conceals it:
here, nearby,
on the old man's crutch-stick,
it would open, as a wound,
into which you'd have to dive,
lonely,
far from my scream, the already also
hewn, white one.

TODTNAUBERG

Arnica, eyebright, the
draft from the well with the
star-die on top,

in the
Hütte,

written in the book
— whose name did it record
before mine — ?
in this book
the line about
a hope, today,

for a thinker's
word
to come,

in the heart,

forest turf, unleveled,
orchis and orchis, singly,

crudeness, later, while driving,
clearly,

he who drives us, the man,
he who also hears it,

the half-
trod log-
trails on the highmoor,

humidity,
much.

TO A BROTHER IN ASIA

The auto-transfigured
cannons
drive toward heaven,

ten
bombers yawn,

a running fire blooms,
as surely as peace,

a handful of rice
expires as your friend.

ORANIENSTRASSE 1

Tin grew in my hand
I didn't know how
to help myself:
I didn't want to mould,
it didn't want to read me —

If now
Ossietzky's last
drinking bowl
could be found,
I'd let the tin
learn from it,

and the host of pilgrims'
staffs
would ensilence, endure the hours.

STREW OCHER into my eyes:
you no longer
live there,

save
on the tomb-
furnishings, save,

pace off the stonerows,
on your hands,

with their dream
paint over the
stamped out
temporal bone's squama,

at the
great
bifurcation re-
count yourself to the ocher,
three times, nine times.

LEAP CENTURIES, leap
seconds, leap-
births, novembering, leap-
deaths,

stocked in honeycomb-troughs,
bits
on chips,

the menorah-poem from Berlin,

(Unasylumed, un-
archived, un-
cared for, a
-live?),

reading station in the late-word,

economical ignition points
in the sky,

crests under fire,

feelings, frost-
spindled,

cold start —
with hemoglobin.

TREK-SCOW-TIME,
the half-transformed drag
at one of the worlds,

the dis-elevated one, intimated,
speaks under the foreheads on the bank:

Quits with death, quits with
God.

YOU BE LIKE YOU, always.

Stant up Jherosalem inde
erheyff dich

Even he who cut the bond with you,

inde wirt
erluchtet

knots it anew, in the *Gehugnis,*

mudclots I swallowed, in the tower,

language, dark pilaster strip,

kumi
ori.

ALL POEMS IN THIS SECTION
TRANSLATED BY PIERRE JORIS

UNWASHED, UNPAINTED,
in Hereafter's
pithead:

there
where we find ourselves,
Earthy, always,

a
belated
bucket conveyor pierces
us cloudtorn,
upwards, downwards,

seditious
piping inside, on Fool's
legs,

the flightshadow in
the iridescing round

heals us in, into the seven-
height,

ice-age-close
the felt swan pair steers
through the hovering
stone-icon

YOU LIE in the great listening
ambushed, snowed in.

Go to the Spree, go to the Havel,
go to the butcher hooks,
to the red apple stakes
from Sweden —

Here comes the table with the presents,
he turns around an Eden —

The man became a sieve, the woman
had to swim, the saw,
for herself, for none, for everyone —

The Landwehrkanal will not roar
Nothing
        stops.

LILAC AIR with yellow windowstains,

Orion's belt above the
Anhalter ruin,

Flamehour, nothing
intercurrent yet,

from
standing bar to
snow bar.

WELL-GRAVES in the wind:

someone will play the viola, day downward, in the ale house,
someone will stand on his head in the word Enough,
someone will hang crosslegged in the gateway, next to the winch.

This year
does not roar across,
it throws back December, November,
it turns up its wounds,
it opens up to you, young
grave-
well,
twelvemouth.

THE BREACHED YEAR
with the moldering edges
of delusion bread.

Drink
from my mouth.

UNREADABILITY of this
world. All doubles.

The strong clocks
back the fissure-hour,
hoarsely.

You, wedged into your deepest,
climb out of yourself
for ever.

WHORISH ELSE. And eternity
blood-black circumbabeled.

Moored
by your loamy locks
my faith.

Two fingers, far from the hand,
a-row the swampy
oath.

WHAT SEWS
at this voice? What
does this
voice
sew
hither, beyond?

The chasms are
sworn in on White, from them
arose
the snowneedle,

swallow it,

you order the world,
that counts
as much as nine names,
named on knees,

tumuli, tumuli,
you hill away, alive,
come
into the kiss,

a flip of the fin,
steady,
lights up the bays,
you drop
anchor, your shadow
strips you off on the bush,

arrival,
descent,

a chafer recognizes you,
you are approaching
each other,
caterpillars
spin you in,

the Great
Sphere
allows you passage through,

soon
the leaf buttons its vein on to yours,
sparks
have to cross through
for the length of a breath-need,

you are entitled to a tree, a day,
it decodes the number,

a word with all its green
enters itself, transplants itself,

follow it

I HEAR THE AXE HAS BLOSSOMED,
I hear the place is unnamable,

I hear the bread which looks at him
heals the hanged man,
the bread the woman baked for him,

I hear they call life
the only shelter.

WITH THE VOICE OF THE FIELDMOUSE
you squeak up,

a sharp
clamp,
you bite through the shirt into my skin,

a cloth,
you slide across my mouth,
midway through my
words weighing you, shadow,
down.

IN LIZARD-
skins, Epi-
leptic one,
I bed you, on the cornices,
the gable-
holes
bury us, with lightdung.

SNOWPART, arched, to the last,
in the updraft, before
the forever dewindowed
huts:

flatdreams skip
over the
chamfered ice;

to carve out
the wordshadows, to stack them
around the cramp
in the crater.

ALL POEMS IN THIS SECTION
TRANSLATED BY PIERRE JORIS

from ZEITGEHÖFT / TIMEHALO

ALMONDING YOU, who only halfspoke,
yet was trembled from the seed on up,
you
I let wait,
you.

And was
not yet
uneyed,
as yet unthorned in the constellation
of the song that begins
star, the song that begins:
Hachnissini

IT STOOD
on your lip : the figsplinter

it stood
around us : Jerusalem

.

it stood
above the Daneship:
the bright-fir-scent, we thanked it,

I stood
in you.

THE SWELTER
adds us up
in the ass's bray before
Absalom's tomb, here too,

Gethsemane, over there,
the outflanked, whom
does it bury?

At the nearest gate nothing opens,

above you, open one, I carry you toward me.

WE WHO LIKE THE SEAOATS GUARD,
in N'we Awiwim,

the unkissed
stone of a complaint
swells up,
before fulfillment,

it palpates our mouths,
it crosses
over to us,

alloyed to us
in its Whiteness,

we hand ourselves on:
to you and to me,

night, be careful, the sand-
commanded
is strict
with us two.

A RING, FOR BOWDRAWING,
loosed after the wordswarm
that founders behind the world,
with the starlings,

Arrowy one, when you whir toward me,
I know from where,

I forget from where.

THE RADIANCE, yes, the one that
Abu Tor
saw riding toward us, when we

orphaned into each other, for life,
not only up from the wrists — :

a goldbuoy, from
temple-depths,
surveyed the danger that
slyly underlay us.

NITIDOUS YOU
tumor daughter
of a blinding in the cosmos,

seized
by supracelestial search troops
shunted
into the seeing, god-
waiving
starheap Blue,

you turn
gamey
before our
hungry, immovable
pores,
an also-sun, between
two brightshots
abyss.

COME, make the world mean with yourself
come, let me fill you up with
all that's mine,

One with you I am,
to capture us,

even now.

A BOOTFULL OF BRAIN
set out in the rain:

there will be a going, a great one,
far across the borders
they draw us.

THE TRUMPET'S PART
deep in the glowing
Empty-text,
at lamp's level,
in the timehole:

listen your way in
mouthwise.

THE POLES
are in us,
insurmountable
while awake,
we sleep across, to the Gate
of Mercy,

I lose you to you, that
is my snow-comfort,

say that Jerusalem *is,*

say it, as if I was this
your Whiteness
as if you were
mine,

as if without us we could be we

I leaf you open, forever,

you pray, you lay
us free.

THE KINGSWAY behind the fake door,

before it, deathed
in by the counter-
sign, the lionsign,

the constellation, keel up,
mired in,

you, with the
wound-fathoming
eyelash.

THERE ALSO comes a meaning
down the narrowest cut,

it is breached
by the deadliest of our
standing marks.

I DRINK WINE from two glasses
and harrow
the king's caesura
like that other
does Pindar,

God turns in the tuning fork
as one of the small
just ones,

from the lottery drum falls
our doit.

SOMETHING SHALL BE, later,
that fills itself with you
and lifts itself
to a mouth

Out of shattered
madness
I raise myself
and watch my hand
as it draws the one
single
circle.

NOTHINGNESS, for the sake
of our names
— they gather us in —
seals,

the end believes us
the beginning,

before the
masters en-
silencing us,
in the undifferentiated, attesting
itself: the clammy
brightness.

IN THE BELLSHAPE the
believing-unbelieving
souls gasp,

star-nonsense
propagates itself, even with my
hand, in desert-sense en-
duned by you,

we got here
long ago.

AS I carry the ringshadow
you carry the ring,

something, used to heaviness,
strains itself
lifting us,
infinite
de-eternalizing you.

STRANGENESS
has netted us,
transience reaches
helplessly through us,

take my pulse, it too,
into yourself,

then we shall prevail
against you, against me,

something enclothes us
in dayskin, in nightskin,
for the game with the highest, epi-
leptic seriousness.

ILLUMINATED, the seeds
which I in you
won swimming,

rowed free,
the names — they
sail the straits,

a blessing, up front,
compacts into
a weather-sensing
fist.

ALL POEMS IN THIS SECTION
TRANSLATED BY PIERRE JORIS

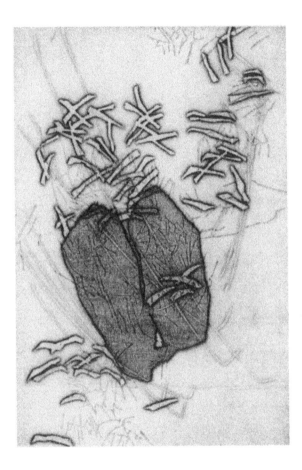

Previous page:
Gisèle Celan-Lestrange,
etching, no. 11 in the series
Schwarzmaut.

CONVERSATION
IN THE MOUNTAINS

One evening, when the sun had set and not only the sun, the Jew —
Jew and son of a Jew — went off, left his house and went off, and with
him his name, his unpronounceable name, went and came, came trot-
ting along, made himself heard, came with a stick, came over stones,
do you hear me, you do, it's me, me, me and whom you hear, whom
you think you hear, me and the other — so he went off, you could hear
it, went off one evening when various things had set, went under
clouds, went in the shadow, his own and not his own — because
the Jew, you know, what does he have that is really his own, that is
not borrowed, taken and not returned — so he went off and walked
along this road, this beautiful, incomparable road, walked like Lenz
through the mountains, he who had been allowed to live down in the
plain where he belongs, he, the Jew, walked and walked. Walked, yes,
along this road, this beautiful road.

And who do you think came to meet him? His cousin came to
meet him, his first cousin, a quarter of a Jew's life older, tall he came,
came, he too, in the shadow, borrowed of course — because, I ask and
ask you, how could he come with his own when God had made him
a Jew — came, tall, came to meet the other, Gross approached Klein,
and Klein, the Jew, silenced his stick before the stick of the Jew Gross.

The stones, too, were silent. And it was quiet in the mountains where they walked, one and the other.

So it was quiet, quiet up there in the mountains. But it was not quiet for long, because when a Jew comes along and meets another, silence cannot last, even in the mountains. Because the Jew and nature are strangers to each other, have always been and still are, even today, even here.

So there they are, the cousins. On the left, the turk's-cap lily blooms, blooms wild, blooms like nowhere else. And on the right, corn-salad, and *dianthus superbus,* the maiden-pink, not far off. But they, those cousins, have no eyes, alas. Or, more exactly: they have, even they have eyes, but with a veil hanging in front of them, no, not in front, behind them, a moveable veil. No sooner does an image enter than it gets caught in the web, and a thread starts spinning, spinning itself around the image, a veil-thread; spins itself around the image and begets a child, half image, half veil.

Poor lily, poor corn-salad. There they stand, the cousins, on a road in the mountains, the stick silent, the stones silent, and the silence no silence at all. No word has come to an end and no phrase, it is nothing but a pause, an empty space between the words, a blank — you see all the syllables stand around, waiting. They are tongue and mouth as before, these two, and in their eyes there hangs a veil, and you, poor flowers, are not even there, are not blooming, you do not exist, and July is not July.

The windbags! Even now, when their tongues stumble dumbly against their teeth and their lips won't round themselves, they have something to say to each other. All right then, let them talk . . .

"You've come a long way, have come all the way here . . ."

"I have. I've come, like you."

"I know."

"You know. You know and see: The earth folded up here, folded once and twice and three times, and opened up in the middle, and in the middle there is water, and the water is green, and the green is white, and the white comes from even farther up, from the glaciers, and one could say, but one shouldn't, that this is the language that counts here, the green with the white in it, a language not for you and not for me — because, I ask you, for whom is it meant, the earth, not for you, I say, is it meant, and not for me — a language, well, without I and without You nothing but He, nothing but It, you understand, and She, nothing but that."

"I understand, I do. After all, I've come a long way, I've come like you."

"I know."

"You know and you want to ask: And even so you've *come* all the way, *come* here even so — why, and what for?"

"Why, and what for ... Because I had to talk, maybe, to myself or to you, talk with my mouth and tongue, not just with my stick. Because to whom does it talk, my stick? It talks to the stones, and the stones — to whom do they talk?"

"To whom should they talk, cousin? They do not talk, they speak, and who speaks does not talk to anyone, cousin, he speaks because nobody hears him, nobody and Nobody, and then he says, himself, not his mouth or his tongue, he, and only he, says: Do you hear me?"

"Do you hear me, he says — I know, cousin, I know ... Do you hear me, he says, I'm here. I am here, I've come. I've come with my stick, me and no other, me and not him, me with my hour, my undeserved hour, me who have been hit, who have not been hit, me with my memory, with my lack of memory, me, me, me ..."

"He says, he says ... Do you hear me, he says ... And Do-you-hear-me, of course, Do-you-hear-me does not say anything, does not

answer, because Do-you-hear-me is one with the glaciers, is three in
one, and not for men . . . The green-and-white there, with the turk's-
cap lily, with the corn-salad . . . But I, cousin, I who stand here on this
road, here where I do not belong, today, now that it has set, the sun
and its light, I, here, with the shadow, my own and not my own, I —
I who can tell you:

"I lay on the stones, back then, you know, on the stone tiles; and
next to me the others who were like me, the others who were different
and yet like me, my cousins. They lay there sleeping, sleeping and not
sleeping, dreaming and not dreaming, and they did not love me, and
I did not love them because I was one, and who wants to love One
when there are many, even more than those lying near me, and who
wants to be able to love all, and I don't hide it from you, I did not love
them who could not love me, I loved the candle which burned in the
left corner, I loved it because it burned down, not because *it* burned
down, because *it* was *his* candle, the candle he had lit, our mothers' fa-
ther, because on that evening there had begun a day, a particular day:
the seventh, the seventh to be followed by the first, the seventh and not
the last, cousin, I did not love *it,* I loved its burning down and, you
know, I haven't loved anything since.

"No. Nothing. Or maybe whatever burned down like that candle
on that day, the seventh, not the last; not on the last day, no, because
here I am, here on this road which they say is beautiful, here I am, by
the turk's-cap lily and the corn-salad, and a hundred yards over, over
there where I could go, the larch gives way to the stone-pine, I see it,
I see it and don't see it, and my stick which talked to the stones, my
stick is silent now, and the stones you say can speak, and in my eyes
there is that moveable veil, there are veils, moveable veils, you lift one,
and there hangs another, and the star there — yes, it is up there now,
above the mountains — if it wants to enter it will have to wed and

soon it won't be itself, but half veil and half star, and I know, I know, cousin, I know I've met you here, and we talked, a lot, and those folds there, you know they are not for men, and not for us who went off and met here, under the star, we the Jews who came like Lenz through the mountains, you Gross and me Klein, you, the windbag, and me, the windbag, with our sticks, with our unpronounceable names, with our shadows, our own and not our own, you here and me here —

"me here, me, who can tell you all this, could have and don't and didn't tell you; me with a turk's-cap lily on my left, me with corn-salad, me with my burned candle, me with the day, me with the days, me here and there, me, maybe accompanied — now — by the love of those I didn't love, me on the way to myself, up here."

· R W ·

THE MERIDIAN

*Speech on the occasion of receiving the Georg Büchner Prize,
Darmstadt, October 22, 1960*

Ladies and Gentlemen,

Art, you will remember, is a puppet-like, iambic, five-footed thing without — and this last characteristic has its mythological validation in Pygmalion and his statue — without offspring.

In this form, it is the subject of a conversation in *Danton's Death* which takes place in a room, not yet in the Conciergerie, a conversation which, we feel, could go on forever if there were no snags.

There are snags.

Art comes up again. It comes up in another work of Georg Büchner's, in *Woyzeck*, among other, nameless people in a yet more "ashen light before the storm" — if I may use the phrase Moritz Heimann intended for *Danton's Death*. Here, in very different times, art comes presented by a carnival barker and has no longer, as in that conversation, anything to do with "glowing," "roaring," "radiant" creation, but is put next to the "creature as God made it" and the "nothing" this creature is "wearing." This time, art comes in the shape of a monkey. But it is art all right. We recognize it by its "coat and trousers."

It — art — comes to us in yet a third play of Büchner's, in *Leonce and Lena*. Time and lighting are unrecognizable: we are "fleeing towards paradise"; and "all clocks and calendars" are soon to be "broken" or, rather, "forbidden." But just before that moment, "two persons of the two sexes" are introduced: "two world-famous automatons have arrived." And a man who claims to be "the third and perhaps strangest of the two" invites us, "with a rattling voice," to admire what we see: "Nothing but art and mechanics, nothing but cardboard and springs."

Art appears here in larger company than before, but obviously of its own sort. It is the same art: art as we already know it. Valeria is only another name for the barker.

Art, ladies and gentlemen, with all its attributes and future additions, is also a problem and, as we can see, one that is variable, tough, long lived, let us say, eternal.

A problem which allows a mortal, Camille, and a man whom we can only understand through his death, Danton, to join word to word to word. It is easy to talk about art.

But when there is talk of art, there is often somebody who does not really listen.

More precisely: somebody who hears, listens, looks . . . and then does not know what it was about. But who hears the speaker, "sees him speaking," who perceives language as a physical shape and also — who could doubt it within Büchner's work — breath, that is, direction and destiny.

I am talking — you have long guessed it as she comes to you year after year, not by accident quoted so frequently — I am talking of Lucile.

The snags which halt the conversation in *Danton's Death* are brutal. They take us to the *Place de la Révolution:* "the carts drive up and stop." They are all there, Danton, Camille, and the rest. They do not lack words, even here, artful, resonant words, and they get them out. Words — in places Büchner need only quote — about going to their death together; Fabre would even like to die "twice"; everybody rises to the occasion. Only a few voices, "some" — unnamed — "voices," find they "have heard it before, it is boring."

And here where it all comes to an end, in those long last moments when Camille — no, not *the* Camille, a fellow prisoner — when this other Camille dies a theatrical, I am tempted to say iambic death which we only two scenes later come to feel as his own, through another person's words, not his, yet kin — here where it all comes to its end, where all around Camille pathos and sententiousness confirm the triumph of "puppet" and "string," here Lucile who is blind against art, Lucile for whom language is tangible and like a person, Lucile is suddenly there with her "Long live the king!"

After all those words on the platform (the guillotine, mind you) — what a word!

It is a word against the grain, the word which cuts the "string," which does not bow to the "bystanders and old warhorses of history." It is an act of freedom. It is a step.

True, it sounds — and in the context of what I now, today, dare say about it, this is perhaps no accident — it sounds at first like allegiance to the "ancien régime."

But it is not. Allow me, who grew up on the writings of Peter

Kropotkin and Gustav Landauer, to insist: this is not homage to any monarchy, to any yesterday worth preserving.

It is homage to the majesty of the absurd which bespeaks the presence of human beings.

This, ladies and gentlemen, has no definitive name, but I believe that this is . . . poetry.

"Oh, art!" You see I am stuck on this word of Camille's.

I know we can read it in different ways, we can give it a variety of accents: the acute of the present, the grave accent of history (literary history included), the circumflex (marking length) of eternity.

I give it — I have no other choice — I give it an acute accent.

Art — "oh, art!" — besides being changeable, has the gift of ubiquity. We find it again in *Lenz*, but, let me stress this, as in *Danton's Death*, only as an episode.

"Over dinner, Lenz recovered his spirits: they talked literature, he was in his element . . ."
". . . The feeling that there is life in a work was more important than those other two, was the only criterion in matters of art . . ."

I picked only two sentences. My bad conscience about the grave accent bids me draw your attention to their importance in literary history. We must read this passage together with the conversation in *Danton's Death*. Here, Büchner's aesthetics finds expression. It leads us from the Lenz-fragment to Reinhold Lenz, author of *Notes on the Theatre*, and, back beyond the historical Lenz, to Mercier's seminal

"Elargissez l'art." This passage opens vistas: it anticipates Naturalism and Gerhart Hauptmann. Here we must look for the social and political roots of Büchner's work, and here we will find them.

Ladies and gentlemen, it has, if only for a moment, calmed my conscience that I did not fail to mention all this. But it also shows, and thereby disturbs my conscience again, that I cannot get away from something which seems connected with art.

I am looking for it here, in *Lenz* — now you are forewarned.

Lenz, that is, Büchner, has ('oh, art') only contemptuous words for "idealism" and its "wooden puppets." He contrasts it with what is natural for the creature and follows up with his unforgettable lines about the "life of the least of beings," the "tremors and hints," the "subtle, hardly noticeable play of expressions on his face." And he illustrates this view of art with a scene he has witnessed:

> As I was walking in the valley yesterday, I saw two girls sitting on a rock. One was putting up her hair, and the other helped. The golden hair hanging down, and a pale, serious face, so very young, and the black dress, and the other girl so careful and attentive. Even the finest, most intimate paintings of the old German masters can hardly give you an idea of the scene. Sometimes one would like to be a Medusa's head to turn such a group to stone and gather the people around it.

Please note, ladies and gentlemen: "One would like to be a Medusa's head" to . . . seize the natural as the natural by means of art!

One would like to, by the way, not: *I* would.

This means going beyond what is human, stepping into a realm which is turned toward the human, but uncanny — the realm where the monkey, the automatons and with them . . . oh, art, too, seem to be at home.

This is not the historical Lenz speaking, but Büchner's. Here we hear Büchner's own voice: here, as in his other works, art has its uncanny side.

Ladies and gentlemen, I have placed my acute accent. I cannot hide from you any more than from myself that, if I took my question about art and poetry, a question among others, if I took it of my own — though perhaps not free — will to Büchner, it was in order to find his way of asking it.

But you see: we cannot ignore the "rattling" voice Valerio gets whenever art is mentioned.

This uncanny, Büchner's voice leads me to suppose, takes us far, very far back. And it must be in the air — the air we have to breathe — that I so stubbornly insist on it today.

Now I must ask, does Büchner, the poet of the creature, not call art into question, and from this direction? A challenge perhaps muted, perhaps only half conscious, but for all that — perhaps because of that — no less essentially radical? A challenge to which all poetry must return if it wants to question further? In other words (and leaving out some of the steps): may we, like many of our contemporaries, take art for granted, for absolutely given? Should we, to put it concretely, should we think Mallarmé, for instance, through to the end?

I have jumped ahead, reached beyond my topic, though not far enough, I know. Let me return to Büchner's *Lenz,* to the (episodic) conversation 'over dinner' during which Lenz "recovered his spirits."

Lenz talked for a long time, "now smiling, now serious." And when the conversation is over, Büchner says of him, of the man who thinks about questions of art, but also of Lenz, the artist: "He had forgotten all about himself."

I think of Lucile when I read this. I read: *He,* he himself.

The man whose eyes and mind are occupied with art — I am still with *Lenz* — forgets about himself. Art makes for distance from the I. Art requires that we travel a certain space in a certain direction, on a certain road.

And poetry? Poetry which, of course, must go the way of art? Here this would actually mean the road to Medusa's head and the automaton!

I am not looking for a way out, I am only pushing the question farther in the same direction which is, I think, also the direction of the *Lenz* fragment.

Perhaps — I am only speculating — perhaps poetry, like art, moves with the oblivious self into the uncanny and strange to free itself. Though where? in which place? how? as what? This would mean art is the distance poetry must cover, no less and no more.

I know there are other, shorter routes. But poetry, too, can be ahead. La poésie, elle aussi, brûle nos étapes.

I will now leave the man who has forgotten about himself, who thinks about art, the artist. I believe that I have met poetry in the figure of Lucile, and Lucile perceives language as shape, direction, breath. I am looking for the same thing here, in Büchner's work. I am looking for Lenz himself, as a person, I am looking for his shape: for the sake of the place of poetry, for the sake of liberation, for the sake of the step.

Büchner's *Lenz* has remained a fragment, ladies and gentlemen. Shall we look at the historical Lenz in order to find out what direction this life had?

"His existence was a necessary burden for him. Thus he lived on . . ." Here the tale breaks off.

But poetry, like Lucile, tries to see the figure in his direction. Poetry rushes ahead. We know how he lives *on, on toward* what.

"Death," we read in a work on Jacob Michael Reinhold Lenz published in Leipzig, in 1909, from the pen of a Moscow professor, M. N. Rosanow, "death was not slow to deliver him. In the night from the 23rd to the 24th of May, 1792, Lenz was found dead in a street in Moscow. A nobleman paid for his funeral. His grave has remained unknown."

Thus *he* had lived *on.*

He: the real Lenz, Büchner's figure, the person whom we encountered on the first page of the story, the Lenz who "on the 20th of January was walking through the mountains," he — not the artist thinking about art — he as an "I."

Can we perhaps now locate the strangeness, the place where the person was able to set himself free as an — estranged — I? Can we locate this place, this step?

" . . . only, it sometimes bothered him that he could not walk on his head." This is Lenz. This is, I believe, his step, his "Long live the king."

" . . . only, it sometimes bothered him that he could not walk on his head."

A man who walks on his head, ladies and gentlemen, a man who walks on his head sees the sky below, as an abyss.

Ladies and gentlemen, it is very common today to complain of the "obscurity" of poetry. Allow me to quote, a bit abruptly — but do we not have a sudden opening here? — a phrase of Pascal's which I read in Leo Shestov: "Ne nous reprochez pas le manque de clarté puisque nous en faisons profession." This obscurity, if it is not congenital, has been bestowed on poetry by strangeness and distance (perhaps of its own making) and for the sake of an encounter.

But there may be, in one and the same direction, two kinds of strangeness next to each other.

Lenz — that is, Büchner — has gone a step farther than Lucile. His "Long live the king" is no longer a word. It is a terrifying silence. It takes his — and our — breath and words away.

Poetry is perhaps this: an *Atemwende*, a turning of our breath. Who knows, perhaps poetry goes its way — the way of art — for the sake of just such a turn? And since the strange, the abyss *and* Medusa's head, the abyss *and* the automaton, all seem to lie in the same direction — it is perhaps this turn, this *Atemwende*, which can sort out the strange from the strange? It is perhaps here, in this one brief moment, that Medusa's head shrivels and the automatons run down? Perhaps, along with the I, estranged and freed *here, in this manner,* some other thing is also set free?

Perhaps after this, the poem can be itself . . . can in this now artless, art-free manner go other ways, including the ways of art, time and again?

Perhaps.

Perhaps we can say that every poem is marked by its own "20th of January"? Perhaps the newness of poems written today is that they try most plainly to be mindful of this kind of date?

But do we not all write from and toward some such date? What else could we claim as our origin?

But the poem speaks. It is mindful of its dates, but it speaks. True, it speaks only on its own, its very own behalf.

But I think — and this will hardly surprise you — that the poem has always hoped, for this very reason, to speak also on behalf of the *strange* — no, I can no longer use this word here — *on behalf of the other,* who knows, perhaps of an *altogether other.*

This "who knows" which I have reached is all I can add here, today, to the old hopes.

Perhaps, I am led to speculate, perhaps an encounter is conceivable between this "altogether other" — I am using a familiar auxiliary — and a not so very distant, a quite close "other" — conceivable, perhaps, again and again.

The poem takes such thoughts for its home and hope — a word for living creatures.

Nobody can tell how long the pause for breath — hope and thought — will last. "Speed," which has always been "outside," has gained yet more speed. The poem knows this, but heads straight for the "otherness" which it considers it can reach and be free, which is perhaps vacant and at the same time turned like Lucile, let us say, turned toward it, toward the poem.

It is true, the poem, the poem today, shows — and this has only indirectly to do with the difficulties of vocabulary, the faster flow of syntax or a more awakened sense of ellipsis, none of which we should underrate — the poem clearly shows a strong tendency towards silence.

The poem holds its ground, if you will permit me yet another extreme formulation, the poem holds its ground on its own margin. In order to endure, it constantly calls and pulls itself back from an "already-no-more" into a "still-here."

This "still-here" can only mean speaking. Not language as such, but responding and — not just verbally — "corresponding" to something.

In other words: language actualized, set free under the sign of a radical individuation which, however, remains as aware of the limits drawn by language as of the possibilities it opens.

This "still-here" of the poem can only be found in the work of poets who do not forget that they speak from an angle of reflection which is their own existence, their own physical nature.

This shows the poem yet more clearly as one person's language become shape and, essentially, a presence in the present.

The poem is lonely. It is lonely and *en route*. Its author stays with it.

Does this very fact not place the poem already here, at its inception, in the encounter, *in the mystery of encounter?*

The poem intends another, needs this other, needs an opposite. It goes toward it, bespeaks it.

For the poem, everything and everybody is a figure of this other toward which it is heading.

The attention which the poem pays to all that it encounters, its *more* acute sense of detail, outline, structure, color, but also of the "tremors and hints" — all this is not, I think, achieved by an eye competing (or concurring) with ever more precise instruments, but, rather, by a kind of concentration mindful of all our dates.

"Attention," if you allow me a quote from Malebranche via Walter Benjamin's essay on Kafka, "attention is the natural prayer of the soul."

The poem becomes — under what conditions — the poem of a person who still perceives, still turns towards phenomena, addressing and questioning them. The poem becomes conversation — often desperate conversation.

Only the space of this conversation can establish what is addressed, can gather it into a "you" around the naming and speaking I. But this "you," comes about by dint of being named and addressed, brings its otherness into the present. Even in the here and now of the poem — and the poem has only this one, unique, momentary present — even in this immediacy and nearness, the otherness gives voice to what is most its own: its time.

Whenever we speak with things in this way we also dwell on the question of their where-from and where-to, an "open" question "without resolution," a question which points towards open, empty, free spaces — we have ventured far out.

The poem also searches for this place.

The poem?
The poem with its images and tropes?

Ladies and gentlemen, what am I actually talking about when I speak from *this* position, in *this* direction, with *these* words about the poem, no, about *the* poem?

I am talking about a poem which does not exist!
The absolute poem — no, it certainly does not, cannot exist.

But in every real poem, even the least ambitious, there is this ineluctable question, this exorbitant claim.

Then what are images?

What has been, what can be perceived, again and again, and only here, only now. Hence the poem is the place where all tropes and metaphors want to be led *ad absurdum*.

And topological research?

Certainly. But in the light of what is still to be searched for: in a u-topian light.

And the human being? The physical creature?

In this light.

What questions! What claims!

It is time to retrace our steps.

Ladies and gentlemen, I have come to the end — I have come back to the beginning.

Elargissez l'art! This problem confronts us with its old and new uncanniness. I took it to Büchner, and think I found it in his work.

I even had an answer ready, I wanted to counter, to contradict, with a word against the grain, like Lucile's.

Enlarge art?

No. On the contrary, take art with you into your innermost narrowness. And set yourself free.

I have taken this route, even today, with you. It has been a circle.

Art (this includes Medusa's head, the mechanism, the automaton), art, the uncanny strangeness which is so hard to differentiate and perhaps is only *one* after all — art lives on.

Twice, with Lucile's "Long live the king" and when the sky opened as an abyss under Lenz, there seemed to occur an *Atemwende,* a turning of breath. Perhaps also while I was trying to head for that inhabitable distance which, finally, was visible only in the figure of Lucile. And once, by dint of attention to things and beings, we came close to a free, open space and, finally, close to Utopia.

Poetry, ladies and gentlemen: what an eternalization of nothing but mortality, and in vain.

Ladies and gentlemen, allow me, since I have come back to the beginning, to ask once more, briefly and from a different direction, the same question.

Ladies and gentlemen, several years ago I wrote a little quatrain:

Voices from the path through nettles:
Come to us on your hands.
Alone with your lamp,
, Only your hand to read.

And a year ago, I commemorated a missed encounter in the Engadine valley by putting a little story on paper where I had a man "like Lenz" walk through the mountains.

Both times, I had written from a "20th of January," from my "20th of January."

I had . . . encountered myself.

Is it on such paths that poems take us when we think of them? And are these paths only detours, detours from you to you? But they are, among how many others, the paths on which language becomes voice. They are encounters, paths from a voice to a listening You, natural paths, outlines for existence perhaps, for projecting ourselves into the search for ourselves . . . A kind of homecoming.

Ladies and gentlemen, I am coming to the end, I am coming, along with my acute accent, to the end of . . . *Leonce and Lena.*

And here, with the last two words of this work, I must be careful.

I must be careful not to misread, as Karl Emil Franzos did (my re-discovered fellow countryman Karl Emil Franzos) editor of that *First Critical and Complete Edition of Georg Büchner's Works and Posthumous Writings* which was published eighty-one years ago by Sauerländer in Frankfurt am Main — I must be careful not to misread *das Commode*, "the comfort" we now need, as "the coming thing."

And yet: is *Leonce and Lena* not full of words which seem to smile through invisible quotation marks, which we should perhaps not call *Gänsefüsschen,* or goose feet, but rather rabbit's ears, that is, something that listens, not without fear, for something beyond itself, beyond words?

From this point of "comfort," but also in the light of Utopia, let me now undertake a bit of topo-logical research. I shall search for the region from which hail Reinhold Lenz and Karl Emil Franzos whom I have met on my way here and in Büchner's work. I am also, since I am again at my point of departure, searching for my own place of origin.

I am looking for all this with my imprecise, because nervous, finger on a map — a child's map, I must admit.

None of these places can be found. They do not exist. But I know where they ought to exist, especially now, and . . . I find something else.

Ladies and gentlemen, I find something which consoles me a bit for having walked this impossible road in your presence, this road of the impossible.

I find the connective which, like the poem, leads to encounters.

I find something as immaterial as language, yet earthly, terrestrial, in the shape of a circle which, via both poles, rejoins itself and on the way serenely crosses even the tropics: I find . . . a *meridian*.

With you and Georg Büchner and the State of Hesse, I believe I have just touched it again.

· R W ·

Previous page:
Gisèle Celan-Lestrange,
etching, no. 1 in the series
Schwarzmaut.

Paul and Gisèle,
rue de Montevideo, 1956.

Paul Celan in his library,
rue de Longchamp, 1958.

Paul Celan and his son at their
summer home, August 1958.

Paul Celan reading at the Galerie
Dorothea Loehr, Frankfurt am
Main, July 18, 1964. (Photos D.R.)

LETTER #1

TO GISÈLE CELAN-LESTRANGE

[Paris,] Monday [1. 7?.1952], ten a.m.

Maïa, my love, I would like to be able to tell you how much I want all this to remain, to remain for us, to remain for us forever.

You see, coming toward you I have the impression of leaving a world, of hearing the doors slam behind me, door after door, for they are numerous, the doors of this world made of misunderstandings, of false clarities, of stammerings. Maybe there remain other doors for me, maybe I have not yet recrossed the whole expanse across which is spread out this network of signs which lead astray — but I am coming, do you hear me, I am coming closer, the rhythm — I feel it — is speeding up, the deceptive fires go out one after the other, the lying mouths close over their drool — no more words, no more noise, nothing now dodging my step —

I'll be there, next to you, in a moment, in a second that will inaugurate time

Paul

All correspondence translated from French and German (letters #3 and 4)
by Pierre Joris.

TO GISÈLE CELAN-LESTRANGE

[Paris] This Monday [1.28.1952] — 5 p.m.

Maïa, my loved one, here I am writing to you, as I had promised
you — how could I not write to you — I write to you to tell you that
you don't stop being present, close by, that you accompany me every-
where I go, that this world is you, you alone, and that because of that
it is larger, that it has found, thanks to you, a new dimension, a new
coordinate, the one I could no longer bring myself to grant it, that it is
no longer that implacable solitude that forced me at each moment to
sack what rose in front of me, to hound myself — for I wanted to be
just and spare no one! — that everything changes, changes, changes
under your gaze —

My darling, I will call you a bit later, at seven, when I come out of
my class, but I will not cease to think about you while waiting to call
you — I worry always, less than yesterday of course, and even less than
the day before yesterday, but I always worry like I have never worried
about anybody — but you know that, no need to tell you —

What I have loved so far, I have loved in order to be able to love you

Paul

LETTER #3

TO ERICH EINHORN

Erich Einhorn was a close childhood friend with whom Celan had lost touch in 1941, when the former escaped Czernowitz with the retreating Soviet troops. In 1962 Celan was given Einhorn's Moscow address — the latter lived and worked there as a translator — by a common friend, and an intense if short-lived correspondence (fifteen letters in all) ensued. This is Celan's response to Einhorn's first letter.

78 Rue de Longchamp(16TH)　　　address from 5 July
(tel: Poincaré 39–63)　　　　　　to 1st September:
Paris, June 23 1962　　　　　　　Moisville by Nonancourt (Eure)

My dear Erich,
Many thanks for your letter!

I hope very much that the eye operation your mother had to undergo was successful. Give her my best wishes — I wish to see her again too in the not all too distant future.

I have just sent you my books: the volumes of my own poetry, two translations from the French (Rimbaud and Valéry), two from the Russian — one of them I also sent, together with "Sprachgitter" to Nadezhda Yakovlevna — , my speech upon being given the Büchner Prize.

From the things I have put down on paper you will certainly be able to see where my life and my thoughts are. (I have never written a line that was not connected to my existence — I am, you see, a realist, in my own manner.)

I'll send you the Fischer-Dieskau records with pleasure — just give me a bit of time. Russian poetry, even recent work, is not difficult to find here, but of course I would be very thankful to you if you were to draw my attention to this or that new publication. — Nice that we both are translators — you see, there actually are no distances. If only I could count Tanja and Gustav among my readers!

My work at the Ecole Normale Supérieure (45 rue d'Ulm, Paris 5) is experiencing an interruption, as I, like my boy, am on school holidays. We will go to the countryside for a few days, in Normandy, to a small place between Nonancourt and Damville, where it is quiet and where there are simple, real people, among them an old sheepherder from Huesca, a Spaniard displaced here with the Republican fugitives. — Recently, when we were in Damville, they showed the movie *Normandie-Njemen*. One stays at home.

I will be able to work for myself again, a new volume of poems, *Die Niemandsrose* [The Noonesrose], will no doubt come out next spring. Each week I'll return to Paris to check the mail — above all for news from the Soviet Union. — And now do let me tell you how much pleasure it gives me to be able to write to you and yours, to be able to wait for an answer — an answer from Moscow.

From the depth of my heart, all the best!

Your Paul

LETTER # 4

TO ERICH EINHORN

Moisville by Nonancourt (Eure), 10 August 1962

Dear Erich,

I hope that my books have reached you meanwhile — I sent you every-
thing you had asked for — except for the translation of Alexander
Blok's *Twelve* of which I don't have a copy anymore (but you did say
that it was available in the Moscow libraries — which pleases me a lot).
Some of what I sent you, my Darmstadt speech for example, will
most likely not correspond to your taste and ideas, I have only sent
them along because, with all its unanswered questions, it documents
how lonely man can be in a capitalist society. You are right when you
say that in West Germany they have not forgiven me for writing a
poem about the German extermination camps — the "Todesfuge."
What I have reaped from this — and similar — poems, is a long story.
The literature prizes I was given shouldn't fool you: they are, finally,
only the alibi of those who, in the shadow of such alibis, continue with
other, more contemporary means, what they had started, and contin-
ued, under Hitler.

In my latest book of poems (*Sprachgitter* [Speech-Grille]) you'll find
a poem called "Engführung" ["Stretto"] which evokes the devastation

caused by the atom bomb. At a central place stands, as fragment, this sentence by Democritus: "There exists nothing except atoms and empty space; everything else is opinion." I don't need to underline that the poem was written because of that opinion — for the sake of the *human*, thus against all emptiness and atomizing.

How happy it would make me if you wanted to translate one or the other piece I hardly need to tell you.

How is your mother? and your wife and little Marina? And where do you spend your holidays?

We will be in Normandy until the middle of September. And hope to be able to spend our next summer holidays in the Soviet Union.

The records you sent me are beautiful. Please tell Samuel Marshak that I truly venerate his work.

We greet you warmly!

Paul

I would be very thankful if, as you suggested, you would from time to time draw my attention to books by the new young Soviet poets, — and please also tell me where I went wrong in my translations.

TO RENÉ CHAR

Draft of an unsent letter concerning the Goll affair.

78 rue de Longchamp

Paris, 22 March 1962

Dear René Char,

Thank you for your so true letter. Thank you for shaking my hand —
I shake yours.

What is happening to me, excuse me for speaking of it again, is, be-
lieve me, rather unique in its genre. Poetry, as you well know, does not
exist without the poet, without its person — without the person —,
and, you see, the hoodlums, those of the right as well as those of the
"left," have managed to get together in order to annihilate me. I can
no longer publish — in that area too, they knew how to isolate me.
You — they exile you into the land of the above, but your true country
remains for you. Concerning myself, I am redistributed, and then they
have fun lapidating me with ... the separate pieces of my self. It
won't surprise you if I tell you that the first to have "come up" with
that are the pseudo-poets. There are many of those among our com-
mon "friends," René Char. Many. — Beware of those who ape you,

René Char. (I know well of what I speak, alas.) In their nullity they consider you a source of images to be added up in order to create a semblance for themselves: they do not *reflect* you, they darken you.* And they have worked hard at undermining our friendship . . . they had a lot of help . . .

You see, I have always tried to *understand* you, to *respond* to you, to take your work like one takes a hand; and it was, of course, *my* hand that took *yours,* there where it was certain not to miss the encounter. To that in your work which did not — or not yet — open up to my comprehension, I responded with respect and by waiting: one can never pretend to comprehend completely — : that would be disrespect in the face of the Unknown that inhabits — or comes to inhabit — the poet; that would be to forget that poetry is something one breathes; that poetry breathes you in. (But that breath, that rhythm — where does it come from?) Thought — mute —, and that's again language, organizes that respiration; critical, it clusters in the intervals: it discerns, it doesn't judge; it takes a decision; it chooses: it keeps its sympathy — and obeys sympathy.

But permit me to backtrack: you tell me that you were able to create the emptiness into which your enemies fall and kill themselves — I rejoice at seeing you so strong, so fortified. As far as my own emptiness is concerned, as far as the emptiness they have been able to create around me is concerned, I see it . . . as the generator of a whole race of creatures that I couldn't name. And these creatures, I see them as very prolific: they multiply and keep on multiplying; for the Lie knows how to perpetuate itself — thanks to the "nymphettes" or, if not, by scissiparity.

---

*To which these last few months has been added a true "psychological action" that aims at my psychic destruction.

Wandering, Exile of the Human to be True . . .

(I know some who'd quote St-John Perse at you and his "bilingual" poet — : there too they believe they can obtain {an affidavit} an argument for their vile duplicity . . .)

Ah, that *layer of snow* of which you tell me! For a long time I too had it! But I turned it into the tablecloth my wife spread over our — pleasantly round — table in order to host . . . so many incarnations of mud!

We remember your first visit, René Char, your words inscribed in your book. Downtrodden grasses stand up again. The Heart of the Second Olympian is among them, as is its bow.

Paul Celan

LETTER #6

TO JEAN-PAUL SARTRE

Draft of an unsent letter to the French philosopher (who had just been the victim of an assassination attempt at his home on rue Bonaparte) concerning the Goll affair. The translation is based on the manuscript and incorporates Celan's variants in brackets.

After 7 January 1962 [?]

Dear Jean-Paul Sartre,

I take the liberty of appealing to you [like so many others] [at a moment] not without ignoring [the] your current preoccupations.

I write — I write poetry, in German. And I am Jewish.

For some years now, and especially since last year, I have been the object of a campaign of defamation the extent and ramifications of which go far beyond what one could call, at first sight, a literary intrigue.* You will no doubt be astonished if I tell you that it is truly a Dreyfuss affair — *sui generis*, of course, but with all its characteristics. It is a true mirror of Germany, the roads — "new" — which Nazism

---

* and they have put much work into sapping our friendship . . . They had much help . . .

knows how to take — in patent collusion, in this case, with a certain "left" with national-bolshevist tendencies, and also — as happens often in such a case — with a considerable number of "Jews" — are clearly visible. (All of this, moreover, reaches way beyond the borders of Germany.)

I know all too well that it is difficult for you to believe this unknown person writing you. Permit me to come, in person, to plead my case before you, documents in hand, this case (which I beg you to believe is [rather] unique.)

I permit myself to join a small piece of writing to this letter. I would be happy to give you everything I have done.

I appeal to your sense of justice and of truth.

[In 1948, when I arrived in Paris,]

The facts force me to [ask you] [to treat] to use, concerning this letter, the greatest discretion. I also ask you to grant me a personal interview.

[No signature]

TO GISÈLE CELAN-LESTRANGE

[Paris] Sunday, 21 August [1965] seven in the evening.

My darling,

Not a very good day yesterday, despite your beautiful Thursday letter and the phone call.

Clearly, this publishing house that sends me, without cover letter, letters addressed to me personally, *opened* — no, that will not do. My question, though "protocolled" *(protokolliert)* by Dumitriu, concerning those "two major American publishing houses interested in my work" (postcard from New York sent by dear Tutti two or three years ago) — : still unanswered.

They needed, those bastards, a well-known German-language writer who could also launch a "Lyrik" series for them — so, with the help of that oh so literary bastard Hirsch, they set a trap for me — and I fell for it, counseled by my "friends" Ingeborg, Lenz, Schallück.

Anyway.

This afternoon, the Cinémathèque again: *October* or rather *Ten Days That Shook the World* (after the John Reed book I gave you a few years back), directed by Eisenstein. The USSR has brought it out of its archives, this movie from before the Stalinist terror, made in 1928, and on the credits, before the pictures, one could read that it was dedicated to the proletariat of "Piter" — the popular name of Petersburg — :

Питерскому Пролетарияту,*

so — I, you know me, I applauded.

— Psst! No reaction!

That's the answer I got, forcing itself on a theater where no one backed up my applause. Yet, there were readers of the *Observateur* . . . But the *Observateur,* that's "Leftism," that's the lovers of the Série Noire, the homosexuals, the Idhec, the hip Marxisms, etcetera, etcetera.

So, all alone, I saw Petersburg, the workers, the sailors of the Aurora. It was very moving, at times reminding one of the *Potemkin,* bringing to mind the thoughts and dreams of my childhood, my thoughts of today and of always, poetry-always-true-always-faithful, I saw my placards, many of them, those that, not very long ago I evoked in the poem I sent you — "Vaporband-, *banderole-uprising,*" I saw the October Revolution, its men, its flags, I saw hope always en route, the brother of poetry, I saw . . .

Then, at a certain moment, at the moment when the insurgents occupy the Winter Palace, it began to desert poetry and to become Cinema, motion-picture shots, tendentious and overdone, the inter-texts became propaganda — all that was History and its Personages had anyway been, from the very beginning, what was the least con-vincing, the role of the Left Social-Revolutionaries was completely expunged — , so then the heart loosened, searched for its silences (won, lost, won again), wrapped them around itself and led me out-side, alone, as I had come in, running the gauntlet between young cinephile gents and young girls "mit tupierter Frisur," with too much makeup, in pants, sort of leftist sixteenth arrondissement, erratic and

*To Piter's Proletariat.

flabby. — But there were some, no doubt, who knew, taking, here too, responsibility for the terrible eclipses.

Long live the sailors of Kronstadt!

Long live the Revolution! Long live Love!

Long live Petersburg! Long live Paris!

Long live Poetry!

Paul

TO ERIC CELAN

[Epinay-sur-Orge,] Sunday 15 December 1968

My dear Eric,

It is a great joy for me to see you succeed so well in your studies — I congratulate you on being on the honor roll. (You see, I had in fact expected as much.)

I find that your handwriting has improved a lot; it begins to be very much your own, and in these days when so many things, and not surprisingly handwriting among them, are becoming depersonalized, it is particularly pleasurable to see a handwriting, yours, gain a firm profile.

I am also happy for your reading. Gorky and Turgenev are naturally human, Gorky before all, the *tone* in which he narrates is richly authentic, the problems he goes at he truly lives them, everything starts from the lived experience, and that's very important. Turgenev is more intellectual, more reflective, more abstract maybe, but still always close to human beings and their preoccupations. Of course the world has evolved since Gorky's and Turgenev's days; but to know them and study them in depth means to be able to measure and appreciate what changes, what evolves, what remains though under a new form, often different and yet at the same time identical. — I will continue to suggest reading matter to you, but soon you will pick your own and I'm certain that you will know how to orient yourself. Think also of poetry, of that poetry that is always in quest for truth and I will help you discover it.

I wish you very good holidays in Austria, and send you big hugs,

Your Daddy

FROM GISÈLE CELAN-LESTRANGE
TO PAUL

[Paris,] 1 May 1969

My dear Paul,

Earlier you told me: Don't you too have difficult hours? Oh Paul, if only you knew! I cannot talk much about it and, in order to resist, I also choose to seem like, to do as if . . . That does not fool me, even if it fools others, and often it is harder afterwards . . . But only the walls of my room witness the hours of my greatest distress.

Work is a refuge for me, the one and the other, together with all the illusions that represents, but I can't and won't deny that it is a help. But engraving is now receding, receding; gouache painting too has become impossible for me after that rush. You know how one can't stand oneself when one is not working and the high price one has to pay for the chance (what would be the right word?) for the possibility of working. I have such a hard time putting up with the copper's silences, as if contact could no longer be established, I am lacking that too right now. Moreover, I am once again not reading, again unable to listen to music. The two cantatas you gave me, barely a month ago, I did love them very much. But I have to admit that today they simply bore me. But why tell you all this? I know so well what you are living through and how much more unjust and evil your fate is than mine. Your phone . . .

I have just put on the Beethoven concerto again, which does touch me very deeply. Bach and his immense knowledge also has that acceptance, that resignation which at times is difficult for me to bear. Beethoven is wilder, more human, I feel closer to the pain and revolt of his music than to Bach's. To listen to Bach one has to be well. At least for me it is so. What I'm saying must be totally wrong. But these last few months I have often felt it that way.

Truly, I am begging you to take the step toward the new apartment with simplicity. Don't let moral considerations or questions of merit enter, please. Why couldn't you work there too? and why would it be worse not to be able to work there? Accept that in the middle of all your difficulties there is yet room for small miracles, try to be able to recognize them. I assure you that they happen, despite all. I know this apartment will not resolve any of your difficulties. I have no illusions on that score and I consider this possibility to live in less arduous surroundings like a very small thing; but small things also have their minimum of importance. A crumb, Paul, this apartment, yes, a crumb it is and nothing more, but still it is a crumb.

Tomorrow I'll go to the Grand Palais. I'll finish the 600 forms for the grading of the pupils. At noon no doubt I'll take myself by the hand to return to the Bauhaus. The Klees are very beautiful, and to see them again will make a few moments come truly alive. Kandinsky gives you a sense of true respect that makes you very small, though there remains the difficulty of approaching his work, which still remains problematic for me. I can't get into it completely.

I didn't ask if you were going to Lutrand's next weekend; it would give me great pleasure if you could benefit from nature a little. Last spring I was very sensitive to it, to the changes in the weather, contrasts that didn't leave me indifferent.

I'll leave you now. I wish you all the best. Try, as I am doing, to also see those things that are not bad; there are some of those. I still don't expect miracles: I have not changed and don't count on them and don't live in hope of them, but small miracles do happen and I recognize them. They do happen, Paul, especially when one doesn't expect them. I wish you many of them, they make life better for a few moments, even a few hours, which is better than nothing. No doubt life cannot give much more, this oh so mean and detestable life.

Gisèle

LETTER #10

TO GISÈLE CELAN-LESTRANGE

[Paris,] Wednesday, 14 January 1970

My very dear Gisèle,

That moment which I can perhaps situate. You know my purpose, the purpose of my existence; you know my reason for being. The "kilodrama" has happened. Faced with the alternative of choosing between my poems and my son, I have chosen: our son.* He is entrusted to you, help him.

Don't leave our (solitary) level: it will nourish you.

I have loved no other woman as I have loved you, as I love you.

It is love — that overcontested thing — that dictates these lines to me.

Paul

*Ed. note: According to an oral communication by GC-L reported by André du Bouchet, PC had expressed this alternative in explicit terms, during moments of delirium, saying that poetry was demanding that he reenact "Abraham's sacrifice" (conversation of Eric Celan with André du Bouchet).

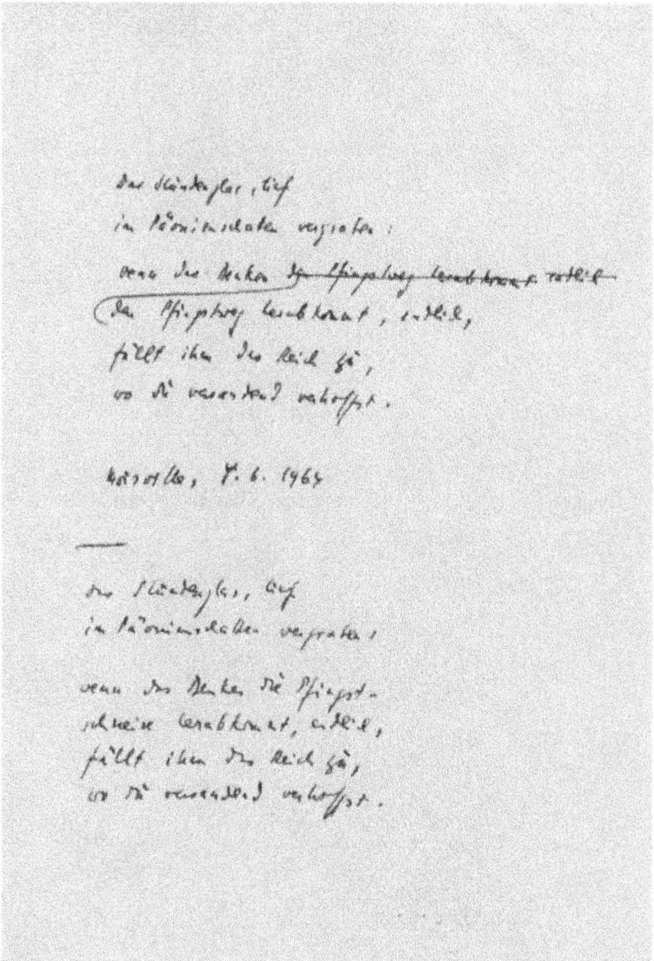

Manuscript, "Das Stundenglas, tief," poem dated June 4, 1964.

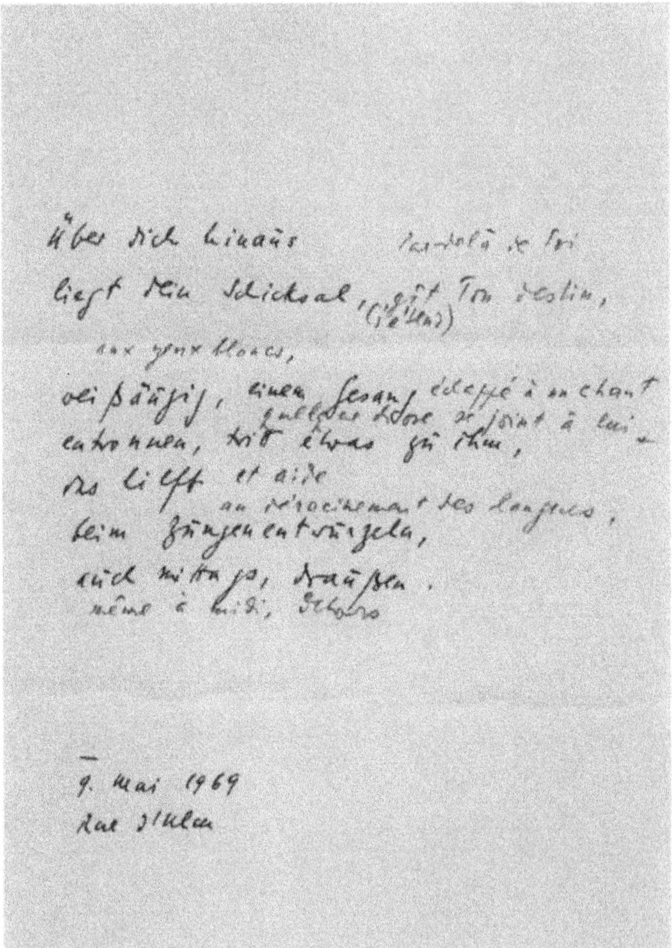

Über dich hinaus

liegt dein Schicksal, (weiß)

weißäugig, einem Gesang

entronnen, tritt etwas zu ihm,

das hilft

beim Zungenentwurzeln,

auch mittags, draußen.

9. mai 1969

rue d'Ulm

Manuscript, "Über dich hinaus,"
poem dated May 9, 1969, rue d'Ulm.

Manuscript, "Es wird etwas sein, später,"
poem dated December 13, 1969.

PAUL CELAN AND LANGUAGE

JACQUES DERRIDA

Q: Would you say that one must have been, like Celan maybe, capable of living the death of language in order to try to render that experience "live"?

A: It seems to me that he had to live that death at each moment. In several ways. He must have lived it everywhere where he felt that the German language had been killed in a certain way, for example by subjects of the German language who made a specific use of it: the language is manhandled, killed, put to death because it is made to say in this or that way. The experience of Nazism is a crime against the German language. What was said in German under Nazism is a death. There is another death, namely the banalization, the trivialization of language, of the German language for example, anywhere, anytime. And then there is another death, which is the one that cannot not happen to language because of what it is, that is to say: repetition, slide into lethargy, mechanization, etcetera. The poetic act thus

From an interview with Evelyne Grossman, Europe 861–62
(January–February 2001): 90–91.

constitutes a kind of resurrection: the poet is someone who is permanently involved with a language that is dying and which he resurrects, not by giving it back some triumphant aspect but by making it return sometimes, like a specter or a ghost: the poet wakes up language and in order to really make the "live" experience of this waking up, of this return to life of language, one has to be very close to the corpse of the language. One has to be as close as possible to its remains. I wouldn't want to give in to pathos too much here, but I suppose that Celan had constantly to deal with a language that was in danger of becoming a dead language. The poet is someone who notices that language, that his language, the language he inherits in the sense I mentioned earlier, risks becoming a dead language again and that therefore he has the responsibility, a very grave responsibility, to wake it up, to resuscitate it (not in the sense of Christian glory but in the sense of the resurrection of language), neither as an immortal body nor as a glorious body but as a mortal body, fragile and at times indecipherable, as is each poem by Celan. Each poem is a resurrection, but one that engages us with a vulnerable body that may yet again slip into oblivion. I believe that in a certain way all of Celan's poems remain indecipherable, keep some indecipherability, and this indecipherability can either call interminably for a sort of reinterpretation, a resurrection, new breaths of interpretation or fade away, perish again. Nothing insures a poem against its death, because its archive can always be burned in crematory ovens or in house fires, or because, without being burned, it is simply forgotten, or not interpreted or permitted to slip into lethargy. Forgetting is always a possibility.

· PJ ·

ENCOUNTERS WITH PAUL CELAN

E. M. CIORAN

Précis de décomposition, my first book written in French, was published in 1949 by Gallimard. Five works of mine had been published in Romanian. In 1937, I arrived in Paris on a scholarship from the Bucharest Institut français, and I have never left. It was only in 1947, though, that I thought of giving up my native language. It was a sudden decision. Switching languages at the age of thirty-seven is not an easy undertaking. In truth, it is a martyrdom, but a fruitful martyrdom, an adventure that lends meaning to being (for which it has great need!). I recommend to anyone going through a major depression to take on the conquest of a foreign idiom, to reenergize himself, altogether to renew himself, through the Word. Without my drive to conquer French, I might have committed suicide. A language is a continent, a universe, and the one who makes it his is a conquistador. But let us get to the subject. . . .

The German translation of the *Précis* proved difficult. Rowohlt, the publisher, had engaged an unqualified woman, with disastrous re-

E. M. Cioran, "Encounters with Paul Celan," in Translating Tradition: Paul Celan in France, *edited by Benjamin Hollander (San Francisco:* ACTS 8/9, *1988): 151–52.*

sults. Someone else had to be found. A Romanian writer, Virgil Ierunca, who, after the war, had edited a literary journal in Romania, in which Celan's first poems were published, warmly recommended him. Celan, whom I knew only by name, lived in the Latin quarter, as did I. Accepting my offer, Celan set to work and managed it with stunning speed. I saw him often, and it was his wish that I read closely along, chapter by chapter, as he progressed, offering possible suggestions. The vertiginous problems involved in translation were at that time foreign to me, and I was far from assessing the breadth of it. Even the idea that one might have a committed interest in it seemed rather extravagant to me. I was to experience a complete reversal, and, years later, would come to regard translation as an exceptional undertaking, as an accomplishment almost equal to that of the work of creation. I am sure, now, that the only one to understand a book thoroughly is someone who has gone to the trouble of translating it. As a general rule, a good translator sees more clearly than the author, who, to the extent that he is in the grips of his work, cannot know its secrets, thus its weaknesses and its limits. Perhaps Celan, for whom words were life and death, would have shared this position on the art of translation.

In 1978, when Klett was reprinting *Lehre vom Zerfall* (the German *Précis*), I was asked to correct any errors that might exist. I was unable to do it myself, and refused to engage anyone else. One does not *correct* Celan. A few months before he died, he said to me that he would like to review the complete text. Undoubtedly, he would have made numerous revisions, since, we must remember, the translation of the *Précis* dates back to the beginning of his career as a translator. It is really a wonder that a noninitiate in philosophy dealt so extraordinarily well with the problems inherent in an excessive, even provocative, use of paradox that characterizes my book.

Relations with this deeply torn being were not simple. He clung to his biases against one person or another, he sustained his mistrust, all the more so because of his pathological fear of being hurt, and everything hurt him. The slightest indelicacy, even unintentional, affected him irrevocably. Watchful, defensive against what might happen, he expected the same attention from others, and abhorred the easygoing attitude so prevalent among the Parisians, writers or not. One day, I ran into him in the street. He was in a rage, in a state nearing despair, because X, whom he had invited to have dinner with him, had not bothered to come. Take it easy, I said to him, X is like that, he is known for his don't-give-a-damn attitude. The only mistake was expecting him.

Celan, at that time, was living very simply and having no luck at all finding a decent job. You can hardly picture him in an office. Because of his morbidly sensitive nature, he nearly lost his one opportunity. The very day that I was going to his home to lunch with him, I found out that there was a position open for a German instructor at the Ecole normale supérieure, and that the appointment of a teacher would be imminent. I tried to persuade Celan that it was of the utmost importance for him to appeal vigorously to the German specialist in whose hands the matter resided. He answered that he would not do anything about it, that the professor in question gave him the cold shoulder, and that he would for no price leave himself open to rejection, which, according to him, was certain. Insistence seemed useless. Returning home, it occurred to me to send him by *pneumatique,* a message in which I pointed out to him the folly of allowing such an opportunity to slip away. Finally he called the professor, and the matter was settled in a few minutes. "I was wrong about him," he told me later. I won't go so far as to propose that he saw a potential enemy in every man; however, what was certain was that he lived in fear of disappointment or outright betrayal. His inability to be detached or cynical made his life a nightmare. I will never forget the evening I spent with him when the widow of a poet had, out of literary jealousy, launched an unspeakably vile campaign against him in France and Germany, accusing him of having plagiarized her husband. "There isn't anyone in the world more miserable than I am," Celan kept saying. Pride doesn't soothe fury, even less despair.

Something within him must have been broken very early on, even before the misfortunes which crashed down upon his people and himself. I recall a summer afternoon spent at his wife's lovely country place, about forty miles from Paris. It was a magnificent day. Everything invoked relaxation, bliss, illusion. Celan, in a lounge chair, tried unsuccessfully to be lighthearted. He seemed awkward, as if he didn't belong, as though that brilliance was not for him. What can I be looking for here? he must have been thinking. And, in fact, what was he seeking in the innocence of that garden, this man who was guilty of being unhappy, and condemned not to find his place anywhere? It would be wrong to say that I felt truly ill at ease; nevertheless, the fact was that everything about my host, including his smile, was tinged with a pained charm, and something like a sense of nonfuture.

Is it a privilege or a curse to be marked by misfortune? Both at once. This double face defines tragedy. So Celan was a figure, a tragic *being*. And for that he is for us somewhat more than a poet.

· NC ·

FOR PAUL CELAN

ANDREA ZANZOTTO

For anybody, and especially for someone who writes poetry, to approach the poetry of Celan, even in translation and in a partial and fragmentary manner, is a shattering experience. He represents the realization of something that seemed impossible: not only to write poetry after Auschwitz but to write "within" those ashes, to arrive at another poetry by bending that absolute annihilation while remaining in a certain way inside it. Celan crosses these entombed spaces with a force, a softness and a harshness one unhesitatingly calls incomparable. In his progress through the obstacles of the impossible, he engenders a dazzling crop of discoveries that have been decisive for the poetry of the second part of the twentieth century, and not only in Europe, at the same time as they are exclusive, impenetrable, stellarly unapproachable and inimitable. They question all hermeneutics, while simultaneously and impetuously expecting and prescribing just such a crisis.

Andrea Zanzotto, "Per Paul Celan," in Aure e disincanti del Novecento letterario *(Milan: Mondadori, 1994), 345–49.*

Moreover, Celan had always been conscious that the further his language moved ahead, the more it was bound not to signify; for him, man had already ceased to exist. Even if in his texts ongoing tremors of nostalgia toward another history are not absent, history appears to him like the deployment of a ferocious and insatiable negation: language knows that it cannot substitute itself for the drift of a destructuration that will transform it into something other, that will change its sign. Yet at the same time, language has to "overthrow" history and something more than history; while remaining subjected to this world, it has to "transcend" it and at least point toward its horrible deficits.

If poetry is anyway always a construction, a composition, including at this terminal moment when everything denies it while traversing it, henceforth history cannot be supported or expressed, neither directly nor indirectly, in its multidirectional flight from meaning. Celan thus expresses himself in a system of forms or a seism of forms, aware that he is moving toward muteness (as he himself on occasion affirmed). This muteness is something different from silence, which can also be a form of realization; it veils and simultaneously makes evident a sort of "arm wrestling" in which an interior force slowly but inexorably ends up gaining the upper hand. Or, more accurately, should gain the upper hand — but there it is: to fall into muteness and simultaneously to find oneself in the same discourse forced into a kind of supreme delirium of discoveries, that is the paradox in which Celan manifests himself.

He advances through the spaces of a saying that makes itself gradually more rarified while at the same time becoming nearly monstrously dense, as in one of those "singularities" physics speaks of. He aggregates and dismembers words, creates a multitude of exacerbated neologisms, deturns syntax without however destroying in it a possible founding justification; he pushes his own linguistic system, German, into its deepest retrenchments. But at the same time he is aware that those marvelous designs of his, those unbelievable "fugues" and "strettos" along scales that may be musical or not, those geologies and suddenly truncated double bottoms, move toward something that is neither an unfathomable beyond of language, nor a return to a birthplace. In each movement of Celan's discourse something insinuates itself — something definitive, lapidary, but of a lapidariness that is like the metaphor for a missed eternity as much as for a death that at any rate remains "worried," un-venged. There are no longer any truly salvational births or returns, just as there is no longer any "Heimat" to which one does, however, aspire absolutely, especially in the context of powerful cultural references, be they the traces of the German tradition going from Hölderlin to Trakl, or the presence of a very deep Hebraic element progressively assumed and borne during his extraordinary and harrowing destiny. One can then say that Celan's fate was at each moment an action, a drama obligatorily sacred (especially in the meaning of the Latin *sacer*) where malediction penetrates benediction in every poetic and human *inventum*.

And his very negation of the sacred, which, in an atmosphere of utter destruction, would in any event remain implied, has, however, always had for him a value of sacredness and intimation, of threat and of seduction, hypnotic and blinding. It was the full acceptance of a destiny at the very moment when that term seemed to have been emptied of all meaning. There remained on the page the trace of an immense effort and of an exceptional gift of creation and love carried by an obsessive auto-frustration that was, however, immensely fruitful and even capable of being periodized in a series of turns, with its iridescent halos of surreality/irreality/subreality. A violence suffered and sedimented onto the page in the stigmata of his terrible rebuses, nearly like the residue of the unnamable massacre.

Other possibilities, other attitudes existed in the face of analogous problems and situations, even if not necessarily as extreme, which many of the highly motivated adepts of our era's experimental poetry have tried. Their premise was to consider givens such as the Celanian experience as in a way included in a kind of sphere to be invested from the outside, to be taken apart and profaned by fissuring it through collisions with a series of psychic attitudes and, before all, with codes that would be profoundly alien to it, borrowed from all the domains of current science (or nescience). It was, in substance, a question of taking apart, of attacking from the outside this "world mode" to gather even the most improbable possibilities for instauring a different relationship between history and the poetic word. For Celan this was an unending problem that he was fully conscious of; though faced with it he could not but feel obscurely impeached, despite his boundless knowledge, particularly in relation to languages, and despite his capacity for ardent symbiosis with other worlds of poetry and experience (suffice it to recall his fervent and complicit relationship with the ghost of Mandelstam). And although all his work took place in close contact with the most diverse forms of poetic experimentalism, including the most "profaning" ones, a contact encouraged by his choice of Paris as elected residence for his daily existence, he had established his exclusive home in the faithful concatenation with a Word which furthermore arose in German, his mother's / her murderers' language.

His prehensile eye and senses, his staggered or stepped pages where poetry "does not impose itself but exposes itself" (as he put it himself), his Mexican sacrificial stone knives, his withdrawals-attacks in the confrontation with language, his procedures, even the most excessive and disturbing ones, are always condemned to gravitate around a "sublime" identity, sublime in as much as empty, and sublime because null. Yet he always remained in the shadow cone of a verticalism, as "in the presence of," as opposed to what could have happened to others. But whatever the place one wants to assign him, it is certain that no one has equaled his poetic richness in our age. It is nearly impossible to follow Celan through the thousands of stations of a Calvary that blossomed into an infinity of seductions, over vast forest flares, over the bites of glacial concretions, disfiguring objectifications, through ambiguous vegetalizations, and a spellbinding history that exploded simultaneously into "parallel" dictions in devastating xenoglossias. But an obstinate force came to freeze every possible resolution around this verticalist non-nucleus, because what, in the final analysis, never lacked in Celan, was the violence of a love that was absolute exactly because it was ever more "without object." Celan could not extract himself from this powerful and terribly monochord attitude to enter into what must have seemed to him like a double-faced terrain playing fast and loose. He couldn't surpass himself (supposing that that would have been worth the while) in this drive towards a form of sublimity, one furthermore disavowed on many occasions, that can be located in the traditions alluded to above and that were "his," from the "Hölderlinian" line and the Hebraic — specifically Hasidic — one, all the way to a "flattening" in the reality, even if the pursuit of "reality" was the task he had from the start imposed on himself voluntarily and had made his own to the point of the ultimate sacrifice of himself.

There remains only to listen to what Nelly Sachs said: "Celan, blessed by Bach and by Hölderlin, blessed by the Hasidim," and to draw from this the arguments for a sincere and pious gratitude to which the whole of our century should pay tribute. And a tribute that should also have been paid to him by someone who had all the necessary titles allowing him to join the poet at the summit of shared knowledge. This admirer, however, buried Celan under a most disconcerting array of attitudes and discourses, wounding him by committing maybe the worst of his many major errors: I am speaking of Heidegger. The poem by Celan entitled "Todtnauberg" (the mountain village the philosopher used to retire to, and where Celan went in 1967 with "a hope, today/for a thinker's/word / to come, /in the heart /") carries the burden of what can be seen as a final disappointment. Even if we don't know much about the details of a conversation in which the fundamental problems of poetry had no doubt their place, he most certainly hoped to hear the philosopher speak his frank disapproval of the genocide or else make some declaration of remorse for having kept silent on the matter. But it was not to be. In the very beautiful and mysterious words of the poem there transpires a Heidegger locked into himself, close to autism, and a Celan enveloped in an anxious apprehension. There remains the feeling of a scission, of a stridence, and as if of a last treason committed by a whole culture against the confident and innocent poet who had risked everything in his writing to set himself beyond absolute despair, without however being able to admit it, and who ends up perishing because of it. There remains the feeling of a fracture at the heart of German culture, or rather of European culture as a whole, which unhappily even today, in a time moving toward a new cohabitation between men, still projects the indigestible traces of a shadow.

· PJ ·

ON PAUL CELAN IN NEUCHÂTEL

FRIEDRICH DÜRRENMATT

Poems became important for me only when I got to know Paul Celan in Paris. We visited him in his Parisian apartment. A woman, painting; a child. He was melancholic, despairing, somber, believed he was persecuted, some German newspaper had criticized or misquoted him, but then when one day he and his wife visited us in Neuchâtel and stayed with us for a few days, we got to know another side of him. We had lodged the couple in a hotel up on Chaumont. At first he was sad, just as I had known him in Paris, we felt oppressed just as we had in Paris, we tried to cheer him up, we just didn't know how to, just as we hadn't known how to in Paris. On the last day his melancholy suddenly cleared, like a sky clears after dark clouds. The day was hot, heavy, no wind, oppressively leaden. We played ping-pong for hours, he had an enormous, bearlike vitality, he played my wife, my son and me into the ground. Then he drank a bottle of Mirabelle, a strong schnapps, to accompany a leg of lamb, his wife and we had Bordeaux, he, a second bottle of Mirabelle, Bordeaux in between, in the pergola

From Turmbau: Stoffe IV–IX *(Zurich: Diogenes Verlag, 1990), 169–71.*

before the kitchen, summer stars in the sky. He improvised dark stanzas into the big-bellied glass, began to dance, sang Romanian folk songs, communist anthems, a wild, healthy, exuberant lad. When I drove him and his wife up to Chaumont, through the late night Jura forest, Orion was already on the rise, then dawn grew inexorably, Venus flaming up, he sang and bawled like a boisterous faun. Later we heard little from him. Once he sent a newspaper clipping, begging me to intercede, suspecting a surreptitious attack, I reread the article again and again, could not find anything, did not understand his suspicion, did not answer him because I did not understand and because I did not know how I could have calmed him without becoming his enemy, given that he saw enemies and suspected plots everywhere. Then he came one more time, from Paris or Germany, as if fleeing from something, sat in my studio between my paintings, was silent, and yet a conversation seemed to get under way, died down, my wife readied the guest room, I went down to the wine cellar, unhappy in the knowledge that I had made him unhappy, that he had sought help without finding it, returned with a few bottles, the studio was empty. Only now do I hear Celan's voice again. More than twenty years later. Suhrkamp Verlag has published two records. I listen to his voice. Celan reads his poems with urgency and accuracy, the tempo even, at times quickening. Word creations, associations, I see images as I listen. Images from Hieronymus Bosch, *The Last Judgment, The Garden of Earthly Delights.* Are these poems still sayable, not too esoteric to have an unmediated effect, hieroglyphs that reveal themselves only after long contemplation, poems of absolute loneliness, spoken behind soundproof sheets of glass, poems without time or tone, black word-holes, word-alchemical? The same helplessness overcomes me that I felt in front of Celan, the sadness he knew how to spread.

• PJ •

THE MEMORY OF WORDS

EDMOND JABÈS

I have never spoken of Paul Celan. Modesty? Inability to read his language? And yet everything draws me to him.

I love the man who was my friend. And, in their differences, our books meet up. The same questioning links us, the same wounded word.

I have never written anything on Paul Celan. Today I take the risk of doing so. I did not make this decision all alone.

To write for the first time on Paul Celan, for German readers, tempted me.*

To write for the first time on Paul Celan and to give my writing as destination the place opened by his language, by his very words, has convinced me to say "yes" — as one says "yes" to oneself, in silence or in solitude. While thinking, however, about the missing friend. And

*Asked to do so by the *Frankfurter Allgemeine Zeitung*.

Edmond Jabès, La mémoire des mots *(Paris: Fourbis, 1990)*.

as if, for the first time, serenely, I accompanied him there where we had never penetrated together, into the very heart of the language with which he had battled so fiercely and which was not the one in which we spoke to each other.

To whom to speak when the other no longer is?

The place is empty when emptiness occupies all of the place.

Paul Celan's voice reading in my house, for me, some of his poems, has never fallen silent. I hear it, at this very moment when, pen in hand, I listen to my words going toward his. I listen to his words in mine, as one listens to the heartbeat of a person one has not left, in the shadow where, henceforth, he stands.

This voice is at the center of the reading I do of his poems; for I can read Paul Celan only in translation; but through the means I have given myself to approach his texts, helped by the poet's unforgettable voice, most of the time I have the sense of not betraying him.

Paul Celan himself was an admirable translator.

One day, when I told him I had trouble recognizing the poems he was reading to me in the French translations I was looking at — there were few of them in 1968 — he said that on the whole he was satisfied with those translations.

"Translation" — as the poet Philippe Soupault wrote in his preface to *Prince Igor* — "is treason only when it pretends, like photography, to reproduce reality. It would mean to decide beforehand that a text has neither relief, nor harmonics, nor colors, nor, before all, rhythm."

It's true; but what then happens to the original text?

The satisfaction Paul Celan expressed concerning the translations, published or about to be published, puzzled me. "It is difficult to do any better," he would add. Is it because, deep inside himself, he knew, better than any other writer, that he was an *untranslatable* author?

Behind the language of Paul Celan lies the never extinguished echo of another language.

Like us, skirting before crossing at a certain hour of the day the border of shadow and light, the words of Paul Celan move and affirm themselves at the edge of two languages of the same size — that of renouncement and that of hope.

A language of poverty, a language of riches.

On one side, clarity; on the other, obscurity. But how to distinguish between them when they are blended to such a degree?

Glorious morning or mournful evening? Neither the one nor the other, but — inexpressible pain — the vast and desolate field wrapped in fog, of what cannot express itself alone, outside and in time.

Neither day nor night, then, but by means of their conjugated voices, the undefined space, left vacant by the retreat of the dispossessed language at the core of the refound language.

And as if that word could raise itself only on the ruins of the other, with and without it.

Dust, dust.

Silence, as all writers know, allows the word to be heard. At a given moment, the silence is so strong that the words express nothing but it alone.

Does this silence, capable of making language tilt over, possess its own language to which one can attribute neither origin nor name?

Inaudible language of the secret?

Those who have been reduced to silence, once, know it best, but know also that they can hear it, can understand it only through the words of the language they work in.

Uninterrupted passage from silence to silence and from word to silence.

But the question remains: is the language of silence that of the refusal of language or, to the contrary, the language of the memory of the first word?

Didn't we know it? The word which is formed by letters and sounds keeps the memory of the school book or of any other book that revealed it to us one day, revealed it, by revealing it to itself; keeps the memory, also, of all the voices that over the course of years — and even centuries — have pronounced and spread it.

Words discovered or transmitted by foreign or familiar hands, by distant or close voices, voices from yesterday, sweet to the ear or cruel and feared.

There is, I am certain, no history of the word; but there is a history of the silence every word narrates.

The words saying only that silence. Theirs and ours.

To interrogate a writer means first of all to interrogate the words of his memory, the words of his silence; to tunnel down into their past as "vocables" — the words are older than us and the text has no age.

For Paul Celan the German language, though it is the one in which he immersed himself, is also the one which for a time those who claimed to be its protectors had forbidden him.

If it is indeed the language of his pride, it is also that of his humiliation. Isn't it with the words of his allegiance that they had tried to tear him from himself and to abandon him to solitude or errancy, not having managed to hand him over to death immediately?

There is something paradoxical to stand suddenly alien to the world and to totally invest yourself in the language of a country that rejects you, to the point of claiming that language for yourself alone.

As if the language belonged truly only to those who love it beyond anything else and feel riveted to it forever.

Strange passion, which has for itself only the strength and determination of its own passion.

Stéphane Mosès notes in his analysis of *Conversation in the Mountains* that in this poem Celan's use of certain expressions borrowed from Judeo-German could well be on his part a challenge to the executioner.
This does not seem evident to me.

The challenge to the executioner lies elsewhere. It resides in the very language of the poetry. A language he has lifted to its summits.
The constant battle that every writer fights with the words to force them to express his deepest intimacy, no one lived it as desperately in his own body, lived it doubly, as did Paul Celan.
To know how to glorify the word that kills us. To kill the word that saves us and glorifies us.
The love-hate relationship with the German language led him toward the end of his life to write poems of which one can only read the tearing.
Hence the reader's difficulty to approach them straight on.
In his first poems Paul Celan is carried by the words of the language of his thought and of his breath: the language of his soul.
He is in need of this language in order to live. His life is written, in the language of his writing, with the words of his life itself and with those of death, which is a further word.
In his last poems the relentlessness he musters against it reaches its peak. To die at the heart of his love.
To destroy what tries to say itself, before saying it; as if now silence alone had the right to be there: this silence from before and after the

words, this silence *between* the words, *between* two languages, arrayed one against the other and yet promised to the same fate.

All his poetry was a search for a reality. The reality of a language? The real is the absolute.

To confront his executioners in the name of the language they share with him, and to force them to their knees.

That was the major bet, held.

If to translate is, truly, to betray, do I dare admit that, in order to hear Paul Celan better, I have taken the road of treason?

But isn't every personal reading in itself an act of treason?

Incapable of reading directly in German, I read Paul Celan in his various translations: French, English or Italian. All acceptable. All insufficient but permitting a better comprehension of the original text. What one lacks, the other helps me to grasp better.

I read these translations without ever losing sight of the German text, trying to discover in it the rhythm, the movement, the music, the caesura. Guided by the accurate voice of Paul Celan. Hadn't he himself initiated me into this reading?

All the languages that I know help me enter into his, which I don't know. By this rare, unusual detour I come as close as possible to his poetry.

Have I ever read Paul Celan? I have listened to him for a long time. I listen to him. Each time his books renew a dialogue the beginning of which I can't remember, though nothing has come to interrupt it since then.

Silent dialogue through words as light as free and adventurous birds; all the world's gravity being in the sky; like stones laid by nostalgic ghosts on the marble of nonexistent tombs; all the world's pain being in the earth; and like ashes of an interminable day of horror of which there remains but the unbearable image of pink smoke above millions of burned bodies.

A nothing rose
a Noone's Rose

A nothing
were we, are we, will
we remain, blossoming:
the nothing — , the
noonesrose.

• P J •

SELECTED BIBLIOGRAPHY

OF AND ON PAUL CELAN

BY PAUL CELAN

IN GERMAN

Gesammelte Werke in fünf Bänden. Frankfurt am Main: Suhrkamp Verlag, 1983.

Gedichte aus dem Nachlass. Herausgegeben von Bertrand Badiou, Jean-Claude Rambach und Barbara Wiedemann. Frankfurt am Main: Suhrkamp Verlag, 1997.

Der Meridian, Endfassung, Vorstufen, Materialien. Herausgegeben von Bernhard Böschenstein und Heino Schmull. Tübinger Ausgabe. Frankfurt am Main: Suhrkamp Verlag, 1999.

Die Gedichte: Kommentierte Gesamtausgabe. Herausgegeben und kommentiert von Barbara Wiedemann. Frankfurt am Main: Suhrkamp Verlag, 2003.

IN FRENCH

Paul Celan, Gisèle Celan-Lestrange, *Correspondance.* Editée et commentée par Bertrand Badiou avec le concours de Eric Celan. 2 vols. Paris: Le Seuil, 2001.

IN ENGLISH

Breathturn. Translated by Pierre Joris. Copenhagen: Green Integer, 2004.

Threadsuns. Translated by Pierre Joris. Copenhagen: Green Integer, 2004.

Lightduress. Translated by Pierre Joris. Copenhagen: Green Integer, 2004.

Romanian Poems. Translated by Julian Semilian and Sanda Agalidi. Los Angeles: Green Integer, 2003.

Poems of Paul Celan. Revised and expanded edition. Translated by Michael Hamburger. New York: Persea Books, 2002; Manchester: Carcanet Press, 2002.

Two Volumes: Fathomsuns and Benighted. Translated by Ian Fairley. Riverdale-on-Hudson: Sheep Meadow Press, 2001.

Selected Poems and Prose of Paul Celan. Translated by John Felstiner. New York: W. W. Norton, 2001.

Last Poems. Translated by Katherine Washburn and Margret Guillemin. San Francisco: North Point Press, 1986. [o.p.]

Collected Prose. Translated by Rosmarie Waldrop. Manchester: Carcanet Press, 1986.

65 Poems. Translated by Brian Lynch and Peter Jankowsky. Dublin: Raven Arts Press, 1985. [o.p.]

Prose Writings and Selected Poems. Translated by Walter Billeter and Jerry Glenn. Carlton, Victoria, Australia: Paper Castle, 1977. [o.p.]

Breath Crystal. Translated by Walter Billeter. *Rigmarole of the Hours, 3.* Ivanhoe, Victoria, Australia: Ragman Productions, 1975. [o.p.]

Speech-Grille and Selected Poems. Translated by Joachim Neugroschel. New York: E. P. Dutton, 1971. [o.p.]

ON PAUL CELAN

Celan-Jahrbuch. Edited by Hans-Michael Speier. Heidelberg: Universitätsverlag C. Winter, 1987. (Eight issues have been published to date.)

Kommentar zu Paul Celans "Die Niemandsrose." Edited by Jürgen Lehmann. Heidelberg: Universitätsverlag C. Winter, 1997. (This is the first in a series of planned volumes of commentaries on individual poetry titles by Paul Celan.)

BOOKS

Blanchot, M. *Le dernier à parler.* Montpellier: Fata Morgana, 1984.

Chalfen, Israel. *Paul Celan: A Biography of His Youth.* New York: Persea Books, 1991.

Derrida, Jacques. *Schibboleth.* Paris: Galilée, 1986.

Felstiner, John. *Paul Celan: Poet, Survivor, Jew.* New Haven: Yale University Press, 1995.

Fioretos, Aris, ed. *Word Traces: Readings of Paul Celan.* Baltimore and London: Johns Hopkins Press, 1994.

Gadamer, Hans-Georg. *"Who Am I and Who Are You?" and Other Essays.* SUNY Series in Contemporary Continental Philosophy. Albany: State University of New York Press, 1997.

Hollander, Benjamin, ed. *Translating Tradition: Paul Celan in France.* San Francisco: *ACTS* 8/9, 1988.

Lacoue-Labarthe, Philippe. *Poetry as Experience.* Stanford: Stanford University Press, 1999.

Nielsen, Karsten Hvidtfelt, and Harold Pors. *Index zur Lyrik Paul Celans.* Munich: Wilhelm Fink Verlag, 1981.

Pöggeler, Otto. *Spur des Wortes.* Munich: Verlag Karl Alber, 1986.

———. *Der Stein hinterm Aug.* Munich: Wilhelm Fink Verlag, 2000.

Wiedemann, Barbara, ed. *Paul Celan — Die Goll-Affäre. Dokumente zu einer "Infamie."* Frankfurt am Main: Suhrkamp Verlag, 2000.

Wiedemann-Wolf, Barbara. *Antschel Paul — Paul Celan.* Tübingen: Niemeyer Verlag, 1985.

ESSAYS

Derrida, Jacques. "'A Self-Unsealing Poetic Text': Poetics and Politics of Witnessing." In *Revenge of the Aesthetic: The Place of Literature in Theory Today,* edited by Michael P. Clark: Berkeley: University of California Press, 2000.

Glenn, Jerry. *Paul Celan: A Bibliography of English-Language Primary and Secondary Literature, 1955–1996.* http://www.polyglot.Iss.wisc.edu/german/celan;biblio/. 1997.

Hamacher, Werner. "The Second of Inversion: Movements of a Figure through Celan's Poetry." *Yale French Studies* 69 (1985): 276–314.

Joris, Pierre. "Paul Celan in English, circa 1989." In *The Poetry of Paul Celan,* edited by Haskell Block. New York: Peter Lang, 1992.

———. "Translation at the Mountain of Death: Celan and Heidegger." In *Poetik der Transformation: Paul Celan — Übersetzer und Übersetzt,* edited by Alfred Bodenheimer and Shimon Sandbank. Conditio Judaica, no. 28. Tübingen: Niemeyer Verlag, 1999.

Silberman, Edith. "Erinnerungen an Paul Celan." In *Argumentum e Silentio: International Paul Celan Symposium.* Berlin: W. de Gruyter, 1987.

ACKNOWLEDGMENTS OF PERMISSIONS

Permission for inclusion in this selection of the following material has been granted by the publishers and individuals indicated below.

Poems from *Mohn und Gedächtnis* and *Von Schwelle zu Schwelle* reprinted by permission of Deutsche Verlags-Anstalt, GmbH, Stuttgart.

Poems from *Sprachgitter* and *Niemandsrose* reprinted by permission of S. Fischer Verlag, Frankfurt am Main.

Poems from *Atemwende, Fadensonnen, Lichtzwang, Schneepart,* and *Zeitgehöft* reprinted by permission of Suhrkamp Verlag, Frankfurt am Main.

Permission to print their translations of Paul Celan's poems was granted by Jerome Rothenberg (for "Corona," "Death Fugue," "Count the Almonds," and "Shibboleth"); by Cid Corman (for "Voices," "Tenebrae," "There Was Earth in Them," "Zurich, Zum Storchen," "Psalm," "Blackearth," "To One Who Stood at the Door"); by Joachim Neugroschel (for "In Praise of Remoteness," "The Vintagers," "Speech-Grille," "Matière de Bretagne," and "And with the Book from Tarussa"); by Robert Kelly (for "Stretto"); and by Pierre Joris (for the remaining translations).

Pierre Joris's translations from the volumes *Breathturn, Threadsuns,* and *Lightduress* reprinted by permission of Green Integer Press.

"Conversation in the Mountains" and "The Meridian" by Paul Celan, translated by Rosmarie Waldrop, reprinted by permission of the translator and of Carcanet Press, Manchester, U.K.

Letters by Paul Celan reprinted by permission of Eric Celan and Editions du Seuil, Paris.

Etchings by Gisèle Celan-Lestrange (*Je maintiendrai;* no. 4 in the series

Atemkristall; no. 1 in the series *Schwarzmaut;* no. 11 in the series *Schwarzmaut;* no. 15 in the series *Schwarzmaut*), reprinted by permission of Eric Celan and Editions du Seuil, Paris.

Photos of Paul Celan (Paul and Gisèle, rue de Montevideo, 1956; Paul Celan in his library, rue de Longchamp, 1958; Paul Celan and his son at their summer home, August 1958; Paul Celan reading at the Galerie Dorothea Loehr, Frankfurt am Main, July 18, 1964), reprinted by permission of Eric Celan and Editions du Seuil, Paris.

Manuscript pages reprinted by permission of Eric Celan and Editions du Seuil, Paris.

"Paul Celan and Language" by Jacques Derrida, from an interview with Evelyne Grossman, in *Europe* 861–62 (January–February 2001): 90–91, reprinted by permission of the author.

"Encounters with Paul Celan" by E. M. Cioran, reprinted by permission of Norma Cole.

"For Paul Celan" by Andrea Zanzotto, reprinted by permission of Agenzia Letteraria Internazionale.

Extract from *Turmbau: Stoffe IV–IX*, pp. 160–71, by Friedrich Dürrenmatt, by permission of Diogenes Verlag, Zurich.

"The Memory of Words" by Edmond Jabès, reprinted by permission of Mrs. Viviane Jabès Crasson.

TEXT: 10.75/15 GRANJON

DISPLAY: AKZIDENZ GROTESK

COMPOSITOR: BOOKMATTERS, BERKELEY